Ocracoke
Its History and People

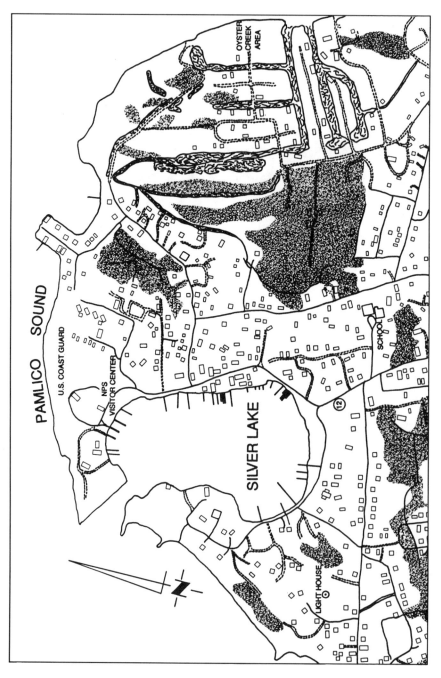

Ocracoke Village map

Ocracoke
Its History and People

David Shears

Starfish Press
Washington, D.C.

Also by the same author:
The Ugly Frontier
Alfred A. Knopf, 1970

Copyright © 1989, 1992 by David Shears
First Printing 1989
Second Edition 1992, revised
Library of Congress Card Catalog Number: 91-75665
ISBN 0-9622806-3-1
Printed in the United States of America
Cover photo by Nick Shears

For ordering information see the last page.

Contents

Preface i
1. Island at Risk 1
2. Blackbeard and Blockades 27
3. The Dowager 64
4. The Man Who Left the Rat-race . . 72
5. The Gentle Guide 82
6. The Activist 90
7. The Controversial Developer . . . 95
8. The Traditional Innkeepers 108
9. The Artist-Shopkeeper 122
10. The Village Policeman 131
11. The Jill-of-all-Trades 140
12. The Lord of the Manor 149
13. The Builder 157
14. The Sparkling Student 161
15. Hutch Minds the Store 165
16. The Teacher-Conservationist . . . 169
17. Epilogue: Concerns of the '90s . . 178
Notes 183

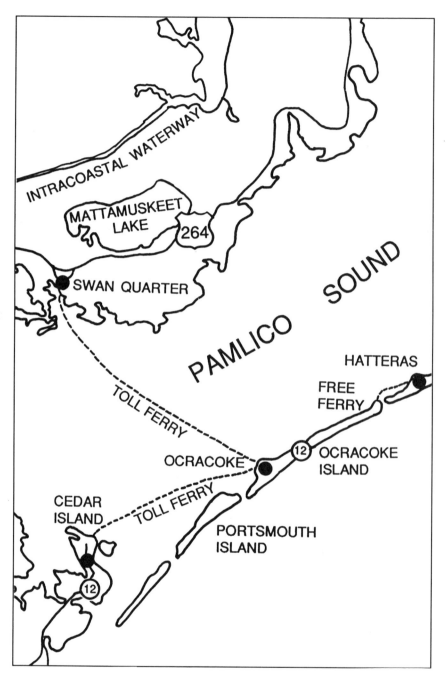

Ocracoke Island and its ferry links

Preface

This book is an attempt to portray a fascinating island that has enthralled me along with countless others. But it is more than a guidebook to one of America's most unspoiled retreats. With the aid of previously unpublished records, it recounts Ocracoke's colorful history — a tale of piracy, shipwrecks, wars, and commerce, followed by decades of stagnation. It also describes the impact of modern tourism on this long-isolated community, showing how mainland visitors and developers have already transformed the island's traditional lifestyle.

To describe these trends and challenges, I turned to the islanders themselves. In a series of interviews, I have tried to capture the diversity and character of Ocracoke's year-round residents. Those interviewed represent a fair cross-section, ranging from those who trace their island heritage back for centuries, to newcomers with remarkably varied backgrounds and reasons for settling on the island.

These islanders offer an insider's view of Ocracoke, speaking openly about their community and the challenges it faces from development, tourism, and other influences.

Almost without exception, the islanders I approached agreed to be interviewed and gave freely of their time. Many lent materials relating to their family history or showed me old records from the Coast Guard and other island sources.

I am also indebted to the librarians of the University of North Carolina at Chapel Hill, the Library of Congress, the National Archives, and the Department of the Navy in Washington, D.C., for aid in my historical research. Mr. Tom

Hartman, superintendent of the National Park Service, and his colleagues both at his Manteo, N.C., headquarters and on Ocracoke gave their cooperation and placed material at my disposal. Finally I want to thank my wife and son, who share my enthusiasm for Ocracoke and backed the project in many crucial ways.

In updating this second edition, I have amended the text and inserted an epilogue describing changes that occurred since the book first went to press in 1989. This new chapter also outlines the issues Ocracokers were raising in the early 1990s, notably their campaign to secede from Hyde County and their drive to become an incorporated township.

A few of the Ocracokers quoted in the interview chapters have moved to other occupations or left the island. Another, the innkeeper Wayne Isbrecht, died in a tragic drowning accident. But I have left these oral history chapters broadly unchanged as these people's words capture much of what is unique about Ocracoke.

My hope is that this book will help foster the understanding Ocracoke needs if it is to survive change without losing its distinctive charm.

Ocracoke, N.C.
July 1992

Chapter 1

Island at Risk

Islands convey a subtle enchantment and Ocracoke casts its own unique spell. It is a place of unspoiled natural beauty peopled by a special breed of islanders whose distinctive character stems from centuries of isolation. For nearly 300 years they and their forefathers have contended with ocean storms that tried to sweep them off their low-lying sandspit. Hurricanes periodically hurled their boats ashore and filled their homes with surging stormwaters.

Ocracoke Inlet was the lair from which Blackbeard, the most infamous and colorful pirate of his day, sallied forth to ravage shipping. After his capture and beheading in 1718, Ocracokers pursued their own brand of buccaneering, plundering shipwrecks for loot to augment their meager subsistence from fishing and farming. Many of today's 700 islanders who live on Ocracoke year-round are natives descended from these early settlers. Related by intermarriage, speaking local idioms, they comprise a settled community unlike the shifting population of most mainland towns and villages.

But Ocracoke has more to offer than a fascinating study in history and sociology. Where else is there an inhabited island that boasts 16 miles of pristine ocean beach untouched

by a single building? For the dominant feature of Ocracoke
is that more than four-fifths of the island, including its entire
Atlantic shoreline, is owned and protected by the National
Park Service. Yet Ocracoke Village, nestled around its little
fishing harbor in the southwest corner of the island, abounds
with motels, summer cottages and restaurants. Thus for
nature lovers, Ocracoke provides the best of both worlds:
unspoiled wilderness and comfortable lodgings. To be sure,
tourist expansion is affecting the village's laid-back lifestyle
and disfiguring its harborfront. But change is gradual even
inside the village limits; Ocracoke has been spared the garish
development that mars most other tourist centers on the
Outer Banks.

Yet probably few visitors realize that behind this idyllic
facade Ocracoke is at risk on two counts. First, the low-lying
sandbar's very existence is endangered, like that of the rest
of the Outer Banks, by rising sea levels. If the gloomier
scientific projections are correct, the entire chain of barrier
islands will disappear beneath the waves by the year 2100.

Second, Ocracoke's traditional way of life is jeopardized by
the island's increasing popularity. Expanding tourism is
bringing in outside businesses and vacationers who are
bidding up real estate prices in the tiny 775-acre section of
the island that is not off-limits to development. The resulting
rise in real estate taxes imposes a heavy burden on Ocracoke's old families, sometimes forcing them to sell out and
break up their ancestral properties.

So far, these trends have done little to erode Ocracoke's
physical and social fabric. Rising seawaters have caused a
few nearby sandbanks to slip out of sight, but the island itself
remains intact. And despite the influx of outside capital,
Ocracoke's permanent population is growing only slowly,
creeping beyond the 700 mark at the rate of about one
percent a year. For the island's simplicity is not to everyone's
liking. Some immigrants from the mainland tire of
Ocracoke's remoteness, bemoaning its lack of medical

facilities and other amenities they take for granted. After a year or two, many move back home or on to Florida or elsewhere. Even many tourists visiting the island for the first time are disappointed by its rustic life, and take the next ferry onward to a more typical beach resort. As Ocracokers say: either you love it or you hate it.

But Ocracoke's devotees appreciate the island as much for what it lacks as for what it has. There are no shopping malls, no discount stores and no typical fast-food restaurants. None of the motels belong to national chains. The island has no giant billboards, no towering neon signs, no drugstores, or movie theaters. It has no golf course, tennis court or bowling alley. Some streets are unpaved sandtracks and its public library is half the size of a mobile home. It does not even boast a traffic light or a parking meter.

In keeping with this modest lifestyle, Ocracoke has just two general stores and one hardware store. The oldest of these, the Community Store, bears a blackboard on its pillared porch to proclaim such tidings as: "Alton and Sally had a 7 lb. 4 oz. baby boy Thursday." In a place where everybody knows one another, Alton and Sally need no further identification. A second bulletin board hangs in the nearby village post office. Since just about everyone comes to the post office each day to pick up mail — there is no home delivery — news gets around quickly.

Tough and resilient, the islanders have withstood many vicissitudes down the years: storms, floods, shipwrecks, wars, unemployment, and poverty. Between the two world wars most men had to leave the island to make a living because commercial fishing had fallen upon hard times. Only recently, with the advent of large-scale tourism, has Ocracoke really begun to prosper. Although fishing is still a favorite local occupation it ranks far behind tourism nowadays as a source of revenue.

Many of the old-timers are weatherbeaten veterans of the sea, men who have spent their lives fishing, working for the

Coast Guard, and manning the ferries. They are described by one mainlander who settled on the island as "characters who talk funny, dress weird, drink a lot, tell some of the god-damnedest stories ... but are as shrewd as hell."

Although they have their share of family feuds and inter-necine rivalries, Ocracokers are generally friendly, welcoming outsiders who respect the island's ways. Long ago they accepted into their tight island community Ocracoke's lone black family, now reduced to one aging man and his two sisters.

Native villagers still tend to speak in a dialect believed to stem from England's West Country, whence many of their settler ancestors came. In times past, at least, some Ocracoke oldtimers would say "hoi toide" for high tide and "what toime is it?" Outsiders accordingly dubbed Outer Bankers "hoi toiders." Such accents are hard to find today, but some peculiar local idioms are still noticeable among native Ocracokers. For instance, when a matter is confused and messy, older Ocracokers say that it is "all mommicked up." They also will call a glassy sea "slick cam," and in olden days the islanders would "pound" a preacher periodically with donations of fish, oysters, clams and other foodstuffs to enhance his meager living.

It is perhaps no accident that Ocracoke's two churches, the Methodist and the Assembly of God, are located on opposite sides of the harbor. For even in this small village there has long been a split between the "Pointers," who live Down Point on the south side of the water, and the "Creekers," who reside "Up Creek" to the north. The split is somewhat understandable. Because there were no bridges over the creek until the 1930s, it was hard to get from one side to the other, and each community had its own stores, schools and churches. Present-day Creekers recall their parents' talk of going to visit Pointers "for the weekend."

This is remarkable considering that the village then was even smaller than its one-mile width today. Nowadays the young dismiss the Pointer-Creeker rivalry as an outdated "generation thing," but vestiges of the division remain.

Ocracoke Village today has its charms, but is not strikingly picturesque. Certainly it does not measure up to the natural beauty of its surroundings. And even its fondest admirer cannot claim that the village has the appeal of, say, Edgartown on Martha's Vineyard or other historic New England whaling ports. True, Ocracoke's handsome 1823 lighthouse, a sturdy white structure set amid lawns, is an artist's delight. The sheltered fishing harbor, quaintly named Silver Lake, is still an appealing centerpiece distinguishing Ocracoke from less fortunate villages elsewhere on the Outer Banks.

With its handsome Coast Guard station, stylish Park Service visitors' center, ferry docks and fishing piers, the harbor is a place to explore. Fishermen work sorting their nets and loading crab pots. Visiting yachts and power cruisers bring a touch of elegance to contrast with the weathered, rusting trawlers. Pelicans perch on the harbor pilings, oblivious to the activity below.

Unfortunately the wider view of Silver Lake has been marred by a tall residential hotel and two massive new motels — one built of brick. Such structures might be perfectly acceptable elsewhere, but on Ocracoke they clash with the island's traditional style of modest woodframe buildings. Also out of place are the occasional mobile homes in the village, some disused and rusting.

The only village quarter with any real historical atmosphere is unpaved Howard Street, a sandy lane with typical old Ocracoke houses nestled under cedars and gnarled live oaks. Most of these early homes still have rooftop downspouts leading to large outdoor cisterns that were once the villagers' main source of water. Adjoining the street lie overgrown family burial plots containing graves of venerable Ocracoke clans that survive to this day: not only Howard, the oldest family of all, but also O'Neal, Gaskill, Garrish, Jackson, Williams, Ballance, Wahab, Fulcher, Styron, and Spencer. At a recent count, thirty-two O'Neals were listed in the telephone book, along with 21 Garrishes, 12 Gaskills, eight Spencers, seven Howards, and half a dozen Styrons and Ballances apiece.

Just a few hundred yards away, beyond the village school, lies the resting-place of four British sailors whose bodies washed ashore after a German U-boat torpedoed their armed trawler off Ocracoke in 1942. The neat little cemetery under the cedars bears a brass plaque on its white picket fence with the familiar Rupert Brooke lines:

> If I should die, think only this of me:
> That there's some corner of a foreign field
> That is forever England.

Britain's Union Jack flies over the plot. Each May a British naval attache comes to Ocracoke to lead the villagers and the local Coast Guardsmen — who painstakingly maintain the graveyard — in paying tribute to the fallen men. It is a touching little ceremony in which the British officer's speech is followed by a wreathlaying and a rifle volley from the sailors.

Sightseeing is the most common reason for visiting Ocracoke, according to tourist surveys. But none of these man-made sights — the lighthouse, the harbor, Howard Street and the British cemetery — can match the appeal of Ocracoke's natural attractions. Tourists can explore the entire village in an afternoon. Unless they are drawn to the beach, the dunes, the marshes, and the birdlife, they soon move on. Some visitors are bothered by insects — mosquitoes, sandflies and occasional wasps — although these are seasonal and seldom troublesome near the water on the breezy ocean beach. Ocracoke, as already noted, is not for everyone. But for each disappointed visitor there are others who return to the island regularly, some of them for 30 years or more. They include dedicated fishermen who visit mainly in the spring and fall as well as the summer tourists who come to swim, surf, sunbathe, and stroll on the unspoiled shore.

From June to September vacationers provide brisk business for every motel, rental cottage, and campground. Restaurants, snackbars and giftshops ply a lively trade and an open sightseeing trolleybus trundles tourists around the island. Local fishermen take charterboat parties out into the Atlantic and Pamlico Sound, and ferry sightseers across Ocracoke Inlet to Portsmouth Island, the celebrated "ghost island."

Portsmouth once rivaled Ocracoke as a busy entrepot harbor for sailing ships bearing cargoes to Carolina from Europe and the West Indies. At its peak before the Civil War, Portsmouth boasted 505 inhabitants, including 117 slaves. Now it is populated only by mosquitoes, its last human resident having died in 1971. But the Park Service has restored several of Portsmouth's historic buildings and its deserted beach is a treasure-trove for shell collectors.

Since Ocracoke is a genuine island unconnected by any bridge or causeway to the mainland, the limited capacity of its ferries saves it from being overwhelmed by the summer tourist onslaught. Even in July or August there are never more than a few hundred people on the beach, mostly concentrated within a frisbee-throw of the lifeguard's chair. Long lines of vehicles sometimes wait at the Hatteras Inlet terminals, where up to eight ferries provide a free service from dawn until after dark. Reservations are advised for the toll ferries across Pamlico Sound from Swan Quarter and Cedar Island on the mainland.

Inevitably there has been talk on the mainland of building a bridge, but nobody on Ocracoke wants this to happen. For such a bridge over Hatteras Inlet, providing a direct link with the highway leading down the Outer Banks from Nags Head, would expose the island to unchecked mass tourism with all the hazards to Ocracoke's lifestyle this would involve.

As a practical matter, the islanders doubt that such a bridge is even feasible. Most of them hope that North Carolina's highway engineers will be deterred by the costly experience of the Bonner Bridge which carries the Outer Banks highway over Oregon Inlet. Hit by a dredge dragging its anchor in a storm, this vital bridge collapsed on October 26, 1990, and remained down for three months. The 370-foot gash cost millions to repair.

Accidents apart, the span is in constant danger from erosion and corrosion. As a result, the state government is likely to think twice before risking more millions on a new bridge along the ever-shifting Outer Banks.

Running the ferries makes more sense. And as long as they remain, the ferries will act as sluicegates, controlling the flow of day trippers and protecting Ocracoke's distinctive way of life.

After Labor Day the island's permanent residents, native and adopted, breathe a collective sigh of relief. No matter how lucrative the tourist season has been, they welcome autumn's approach and the strangers' departure. One by one the tourist facilities will close down until the following summer. Except for visiting sport fishermen, the Ocracokers will finally have the place to themselves. Most islanders agree that fall, winter and early spring are their favorite seasons, when only crabs and fish swim in Ocracoke's waters.

In an earlier era Ocracoke used to attract wealthy sportsmen. They would make the slow journey across from the North Carolina mainland aboard the daily mailboat and stay in traditional hotels or spartan hunting clubs. Some would go out with local boatmen to fish; others would rise before the winter dawn to accompany local guides to shooting blinds and lie in wait for ducks, brant, and geese.

Before and between the two world wars these game birds migrated to Ocracoke and neighboring islands by the thousand, stopping to feed upon the thick blanket of eelgrass along the water's edge. But the eelgrass suffered a mysterious blight in the 1930s and is only slowly coming back. Furthermore, Kent Turner, chief naturalist at the regional Park Service headquarters in Manteo, N.C., says that with the loss of breeding-grounds in Canada and elsewhere there are simply fewer ducks and geese in the flyways than in earlier decades.

Local hunting guides say that many of the geese that still come down the Eastern seaboard feed on seed left for them on the shores of Chesapeake Bay. For all these reasons, few of these game fowl are migrating as far south as Ocracoke these days, and experts say that duckhunting probably never will return to the island on its former scale. Ocracoke's hunting clubs that had been built outside the present confines of the village were torn down when the Park Service took over the bulk of the island in the 1950s. Like other private property, they were bought up in the process of creating the National Seashore.

The sport fishermen who flock to Ocracoke today are of another stamp. Typical of the surfcasters who come to the island — mostly for the weekend — are small businessmen from the mainland. They take the ferry across the Sound and drive to the beach in pickup trucks or vans, sometimes emblazoned with the names of North Carolina tradesmen's firms. Their vehicles contain coolers stocked with bait, food, and beer. Choosing a likely spot, they park their four-wheel-drive vehicles facing the ocean and cast with rods carried in holders on the front bumper. Mostly men, they then spend the day sitting in folding chairs quaffing beer and watching for a telltale twitch on their lines. For surfcasters the most coveted catch is red drum (known elsewhere as channel bass), along with trout, flounder, pompano, sea mullet, and bluefish. Farther out, close to the Gulf Stream, deepsea

9

anglers go after albacore, large blues, tuna, king mackerel, sailfish, and marlin that can weigh up to 800 pounds.

Yet most of the time outside the summer tourist season Ocracoke beach is chiefly inhabited by an ever-changing array of wildlife. Brown pelicans glide effortlessly over the swell just beyond the breakers, often in pairs, and occasionally in long lines. Their long bills tilt downward as they scan the water for fish. Somehow these great birds manage to follow the undulating waves without visibly moving their wings. Yet when they soar high above the ocean they have a clumsy, prehistoric look. And they are vulnerable to gales; after hurricanes hit Ocracoke the shore is littered with dead pelicans. Windblown sand makes pathetic little mounds over each bird's decomposing bones and feathers.

But fortunately the species has made a notable comeback after being decimated by DDT and other pesticides used in the 1950s and early 1960s. And even when pelicans are scarce on Ocracoke beach, they usually can be seen lined up like an honor guard on a tiny sandbank close to Hatteras that the ferries pass on their zigzag course through the marked channel.

Sometimes hundreds of cormorants chase down the coast in endless dotted lines, playing follow-the-leader as they rise and fall in gently curving procession. Squadron after squadron they come, black silhouettes against the pale winter sky, thin necks straining and wings beating madly as if each bird is trying to race its rivals. Contrasting with the cormorants' frantic haste is the relaxed motion of the dolphins, whose glistening black backs arch out of the ocean surface as they gambol on their southward run. Somehow at Ocracoke the dolphins always seem to be heading south and their schools keep regular hours: they normally appear but once a day, usually at mid-morning.

Gleaming white terns nest by the hundred on the sandflats close to the southern end of the island in the spring. Skimmers, too, lay their speckled eggs at intervals along the dunes. Even in midsummer, sunbathers may be rewarded with the enthralling sight of a black skimmer flying just above the water's edge, scooping a tiny trench in the sand with its open red bill as it searches for sustenance. When the skimmer meets an obstacle it simply detours out over the surf until it can return to its precision flying. Agile sanderlings and other sandpipers congregate in groups wherever the incoming waves leave tiny crustaceans like grains of rice on the wet sand. They chase ahead to seize their prey before it burrows out of sight, then scamper back to escape the next advancing wave. Nature lovers enjoy watching the football-shaped mole crabs, just over an inch long, burying themselves in the shifting sand each time they are left exposed.

Further inshore stand stout regiments of gulls, stolidly facing the wind. Only occasionally do the gulls take off to escape an intruder or conduct dive-bombing sorties at sea. Then they are exciting to observe as they pursue their frenzied assaults, splashing the sea with columns of spray as they plunge after their glistening silver quarry. Meanwhile pairs of red-billed black oystercatchers strut the sands close to the dunes, faithfully monogamous and ready to warn their mates of approaching danger with a piercing screech.

Ghost crabs and sand fiddlers dig deep holes and leave their untidy trails along wide stretches of the beach. It takes a sharp-eyed observer to spot the almost translucent ghost crab against the sand before it takes fright and slithers sideways to its escape hatch. Among the dunes, tall grasses and waving sea oats compete with pennywort and beach morning glory for a footing in the windblown sands.

Spanish horses of mysterious origin roamed Ocracoke before there was any recorded colonial settlement of the island. The descendants of these "Banker" (Outer Banks) ponies have now been corralled into a 200-acre enclosure that has become a favorite tourist attraction outside the village. A Park Service plaque at the roadside viewing stand notes the prevailing local belief that the original horses of the herd survived a shipwreck on the Ocracoke coast. It theorizes that the animals came from Sir Richard Grenville's ship *Tiger* which ran aground when trying to enter Ocracoke Inlet in 1585. The plaque explains: "It was common practice to carry livestock on deck, and when no wharves were available, they were shoved overboard to swim ashore." This could have happened at Ocracoke, but the Park Service says that the horses might then have been rounded up and taken to the settlement on Roanoke Island that became the Lost Colony.

Thus the mystery of the horses' origin remains. Rival theories include speculation that the Spanish mustangs came from a shipwrecked Spanish galleon. But whatever their ancestry, more than 200 of these horses — or even 2,000, according to one account — used to range freely all over the island. They pawed holes in the sand for brackish drinking water and browsed on saltgrass and boughs of live oak and cedar.

The horses thrived so successfully that they became a nuisance, molesting village gardens. But they were also a commercial asset since they could be sold on the mainland. So every Fourth of July the islanders would stage a "pony penning" — an island-wide roundup in which a large group of horsemen would ride to the north end of the island to drive the ponies southward toward the village. Sometimes a balky animal would wade half a mile out into the shallow Sound and have to be headed back inshore. Once corralled in large pens at the village, selected horses would be singled out for sale.

In the 1950s, Ocracoke's Boy Scout Troop 290 bore the distinction of being the only mounted scout troop in the nation. Each boy was responsible for catching and taming his own pony. At that time the Park Service wanted to remove the entire herd from the island because of the damage the horses were causing to the dunes and vegetation. Led by the then Ocracoke school principal, Theodore Rondthaler, and his wife Alice, the islanders protested so strongly that the Park Service relented. It agreed to retain a dozen or so of the ponies provided they were fenced in to keep them off the dunes and the island's open highway. Park Service rangers now water and feed the horses regularly. But many nostalgic Ocracokers regret the passing of the Fourth of July tradition.

Halfway between the pony pen and the village stands a miniature maritime forest, where loblolly pines raise their bushy pincushion heads above a mass of beach myrtle shrubs, cedars, and yaupon trees. (Leaves of the yaupon, a member of the holly family, were used by both Indians and white settlers in earlier centuries to brew an ersatz tea.) This maritime forest, containing varied undergrowth as well as trees, was chosen by the Park Service as the site of a self-guided nature trail. From its high point on a sandy "hammock" (a hillock), the visitor can view Ocracoke's wide expanses of marshland dotted with patches of black needle rush amid the salt marsh cordgrass. And at the far end of the loop trail stands a lookout platform from which birdwatchers can observe white egrets and stately blue herons wading in the creeks leading out to the Sound.

At sunset the sky is often enlivened by flight after flight of ibises, proceeding in ragged lines with skinny necks outstretched. To city dwellers shut in by buildings and trees, Ocracoke's "big sky" sunsets are spectacular. Tourists photograph the shifting panorama as the scarlet sun suffuses the clouds with changing hues. As the sun dips into the Sound beyond Portsmouth Island, the deepening dusk is broken only by the steady light from Ocracoke lighthouse. Then on a clear night the stars sparkle against a velvet blackness.

But of course Ocracoke has its share of foul weather. When squalls blow up they can usually be spotted at a distance.

Ocracoke

Sometimes several distinct rainstorms may be sighted at once on the horizon, and they can hit the island with considerable force. Weather forecasts, especially hurricane warnings, are taken very seriously on the island.

Some Ocracokers dutifully evacuate to the mainland when the weather radio warns of a full-scale hurricane. But they leave their homes reluctantly. They are gloomily aware that they may have to wait several days after the storm's passage before being allowed to return. While on the mainland, they chafe with frustration, uncertain whether their homes have been flooded and their roofs torn by winds and flying debris. So in any storm short of a hurricane — defined as a storm with winds exceeding 74 m.p.h. — they generally stay put.

Their forefathers, lacking the ferries and the hurricane warning systems of today, had no choice but to hoist their boats, board up their windows and hope for the best. In their isolation, lacking rapid communication with the mainland, Ocracokers could only crouch and pray as gales lashed their homes. Often roofs blew off, walls collapsed and floodwaters inundated downstairs rooms. To this day, some Ocracoke homes have hatches in their floorboards to enable rising waters to well up without lifting the house from its foundations.

Perhaps the most telling local accounts of hurricanes are contained in these terse inscriptions found on the wall of an abandoned Ocracoke house. Judging from their laconic style, they were written by a seaman used to making entries in a ship's log. They are reprinted here in full, exactly as he wrote:

Hurricane, Sept. 15-17, 1933
Worst storm in memory of oldest living inhabitant. Winds estimated at Hatteras at 122 mph. Barometer fell to 28.28 — lowest known locally. Saturday a.m. Sept. 16 — Tide flooded island. Many people took refuge in lighthouse. Water stood 7 inches above floor in this cottage. Porch torn off by

wind and tide and demolished. Roof over cistern blown off. Fence swept away. Surf against front of house reached the eaves. Worst damage ever to trees. No lives lost on Ocracoke.

Hurricane, Sept. 14, 1944

Storm warning Sept 13, 1944. Day calm and hot. In evening, 14 fishboats came into (Silver) Lake for shelter.

Sept. 14.

5 am. Winds rising: northeast. 7 am Winds reached 75 knots. Anemometer on water tower at Naval Base carried away. Later wind estimated at 100 knots. Barometer 28.40.

7.30 am. Winds shift to northwest. 14 foot tides. Island completely under water. Most fishing boats blown far ashore, causing considerable damage to boats and docks. Mailboat tossed ashore close to coffee shop (Island Inn). Six houses completely demolished. Pamlico Inn damaged beyond repair. Extensive damage done to Gary Bragg's home. 3 feet of water pounding through this cottage. Porch blown off and front windows shattered, and front door blown in. Practically all furniture upturned and much of it washed into kitchen. Kitchen window smashed. Front room floor torn up.

9.25 am. Wind velocity dropped. Completely calm by 12.30 pm. Far worst storm ever to strike island. No lives lost.

Fortunately hurricanes such as these hit Ocracoke comparatively rarely. At the time of writing, the last hurricane to strike the island was Gloria in 1985, followed by a tropical storm named Charlie in the ensuing year. Neither caused devastation to compare with the historic storms of '33 and '44. Ocracoke escaped the brunt of the great Ash Wednesday storm of March 7, 1962, one of the worst ever to hit the Outer Banks. It caused immense damage to resorts further north along the Outer Banks and along the mid-Atlantic coast.

Ocracokers say that — touch wood — they have never had

a single recorded fatality from any of the hurricanes that have struck their vulnerable sandbank. Local fishermen have drowned in storms at sea but the islanders claim that no one has ever been killed on shore. In view of the hazards confronting Ocracoke, this record is miraculous. For like the Netherlands, the Outer Banks are low-lying, averaging only three to four feet above mean sea level. Parts of Ocracoke, notably in the Oyster Creek area fronting Pamlico Sound, stand a mere 20 inches above the water. But unlike the Dutch, the Outer Bankers have built no massive artificial dikes; certainly their barrier islands have nothing to compare with Holland's gigantic system of concrete barriers designed to prevent a recurrence of the flood disaster which killed over 1,700 Zeeland residents in 1953.

Thus Ocracoke lies terribly exposed, like the rest of the thin chain of barrier islands to which it belongs. Its people know that whenever a major hurricane coincides with a high spring tide the combination is particularly lethal. Ocean waves along the Outer Banks that normally rise no more than two or three feet can then reach the daunting height of 30 feet. The 1962 Ash Wednesday storm brought waves even higher than this. Millions of tons of water come roaring ashore, battering down dunes and everything else in their path as they wash across the Banks.

The Atlantic is not the sole enemy, nor even necessarily the most dangerous one. When hurricanes come, their shifting winds send the waters of Pamlico Sound surging from one end of the 100-mile-long lagoon to the other. The resulting floods from the normally sheltered Sound can be more devastating to Ocracoke than the crashing ocean breakers. And only the newer houses in the village are built on tall pilings for safety; most of the older homes are close to the ground, mounted on nothing but a few cinder blocks or bricks.

Hurricanes and storms are not the only natural hazards threatening Ocracoke, for the fragile barrier islands are also at the mercy of rising sea levels. Scientists believe that the Outer Banks were created after the last glaciation period which ended some 14,000 years ago. At that time the sea level was so low that the Carolina coast extended some 50 miles further out into the Atlantic than it does today. Then as the melting ice raised the level of the sea, the ocean broke through the coastal dunes and began creating Pamlico Sound. The narrow dune ridge remained as a bar that trapped sand and sediment brought by ocean waves and mainland rivers. Thus the long and narrow sandbanks were slowly built up into the continuous chain of islands we know today. As vegetation developed, it helped to stabilize the sandspits. But as the sea level continued to rise, the Outer Banks began creeping toward the mainland. Storm waters periodically surged across the low-lying land to scour out new inlets. In this process, known as overwash, sand was deposited on the western side of the islands. Thus erosion on the ocean flank has been balanced by a buildup of sediment on the sound shore of the Outer Banks. Naturalists say that the barrier islands are "dynamic" and migrating steadily westward.

As noted, the rising sea level is not only moving the Banks inshore; it also threatens their very existence. In the not-so-long run — scientists estimate decades rather than centuries — the upward creep in sea level may cause Ocracoke to vanish beneath the waves.

As Tom Hartman, the National Park Service superintendent of the Cape Hatteras National Seashore, bluntly put it to an Ocracoke visitor: "You may not have an island." He was citing predictions by the U.S. Environmental Protection Agency that the warming "greenhouse effect" of carbon dioxide buildup in the atmosphere will raise the sea level by up to seven feet by the year 2100. Hartman's Manteo, N.C., headquarters characterized the risk this way in an official report:

17

There is a growing consensus among climatologists that a global rise in temperature resulting from increased atmospheric carbon dioxide will greatly accelerate sea level rise through melting of polar ice and thermal expansion. Current models indicate that sea level, in recent past rising one foot per century, may rise four to seven feet over the next century. Obviously, this will have a tremendous impact on barrier island and coastal management.

Like King Canute, both the federal government and the state of North Carolina have learned to their cost that they cannot fight the waves — not on the Outer Banks, anyway. Back in the early 1930s the North Carolina authorities set about building oceanfront dunes all the way down the barrier islands from the Virginia border to Ocracoke. They erected fences to catch blowing sand and planted sea oats along with tough beach grasses to stabilize the rising dunes.

After 1936, when the federal government began to establish the National Seashore, the task was handed over to the Civilian Conservation Corps and the Works Progress Administration. And in the 1950s and 1960s the National Park Service spent vast sums on dune-building by bulldozing sand and planting millions of grass seedlings. At one stage in the early 1960s the U.S. Army Corps of Engineers proposed building a massive two-level sand dike along Ocracoke's entire ocean beach. The taller ridge would have risen 11 feet, and the lower one seven feet, above mean sea level. The base of these artificial dunes would have been up to 300 feet wide. In addition, the Corps proposed to build a separate barrier 9,700 feet long to protect Ocracoke Village from the sound side. The $2 million plan drew strong support at the time from both the Park Service and North Carolina's Department of Water Resources. Indeed, the Park Service wanted the dike to be two feet higher than the 11-foot level the Corps had suggested.

However, the destructive Ash Wednesday storm of 1962 convinced many people that man-made dunes and sand dikes could not protect beachfront development in the face of hurricanes. It not only caused $300 million in damage; it eroded beaches back to the dune lines and in some cases exposed sand fences that had been laid 30 years earlier by the dune-builders. It also triggered pioneering studies of beach erosion by such experts as Robert Dolan, a coastal geologist at the University of Virginia. Dolan argued that by trapping large amounts of sand the artificial dunes had frustrated the natural overwash process. As a result, he found that Ocracoke's beaches had narrowed to about 75 yards width since the artificial dunes were built. By contrast, the beaches at Cape Lookout, a virgin stretch of the Outer Banks south of Ocracoke, still remained anywhere from 125 to 200 yards wide. Between 1970 and 1973 Dolan and his colleague Paul J. Godfrey of the University of Massachusetts wrote successive scientific papers urging that large-scale dune stabilization projects be abandoned. They argued that the barrier islands were intrinsically unstable and that artificial dune-building schemes actually served to destroy beaches, not protect them. They also found that man-made dunes disturbed the natural vegetation of the barrier islands.

Impressed by these reports, the Park Service took the scientists' advice. In a major switch, it decided in 1973 to abandon its costly and largely ineffective efforts to build artificial dunes. As a matter of general policy, the government would let nature take its course. Inevitably the decision raised a hullabaloo: landowners, motel keepers, homeowners, and developers from Kitty Hawk to Hatteras protested that their properties were being allowed to fall into the ocean. But their complaints found little sympathy on the mainland, where environmentalists retorted that it served them right for building so close to the beach. Ocracoke was less affected since it had no motels or restaurants on the beach and its village was prudently set well back from the

19

Atlantic shore.

Human nature being what it is, nobody on Ocracoke seems unduly worried either by periodic hurricanes or Cassandra warnings that rising sea levels spell the island's doom. Both the present islanders and outside investors seem convinced that after so many centuries of withstanding marine assaults, Ocracoke will survive for the foreseeable future. And they appear skeptical of long-term scientific projections. At all events, they doubt that the island will die before they do — and evidently other residents of the Outer Banks feel the same way. Certainly Ocracoke is very much alive at present. The sound of the builder's hammer is heard throughout the village as new houses rise and businesses expand. Mainlanders who have bought second homes on the island are renting them to summer visitors for up to $1,500 a week. The Coast Guard and the Park Service provide the island with a steady income of well over a million dollars a year in salaries, pension payments, and purchases of local supplies.

Ocracoke's appeal to both tourists and investors is being enhanced by improvements in utility services. The island has long been plagued by frequent power blackouts, usually lasting for several hours. Even now, the overhead cables that bring electricity down the Outer Banks from the mainland are liable to storm damage. Their power supply, while growing, barely keeps abreast of expanding demand. So Ocracoke in 1990 more than doubled its own backup generating plant's capacity to bear peak loads and produce emergency power. Meanwhile, the island's main consumers are building their own standby generators.

The water system, which until 1987 was unable to meet Ocracoke's summer needs in terms of either quantity or quality, also has been vastly improved. After many delays and setbacks, its plant that pumps and filters water from underground wells has been enlarged. It, too, installed a backup generator. But demand still outran supply, and only after further expansion of capacity in 1992 was the plant due to lift a moratorium on service for new customers.

With these improvements in public services Ocracoke property has become even more attractive to outsiders. One real estate agent says that three kinds of mainlanders are buying property: upper middle class families seeking escape, retirees with life savings, and "those with the big bucks." The last category includes businessmen who fly into Ocracoke's 3,000-foot airstrip aboard private planes for the weekend. Yet most of these investors are buying vacation homes and rental properties rather than moving to Ocracoke as year-round residents.

But even though the population is growing only gradually, the influx of outside money is putting the island's traditional character at risk in both subtle and not-so-subtle ways. On the consumer front, one or two trendy little boutiques have sprung up to cater (with mixed success) to "yuppie" demand for New York sportswear. Craft shops no longer sell only island products such as traditional carved decoys; they now import fancy pottery and other artworks from the mainland. Several Ocracoke motels have also built swimming pools, a move which strikes many islanders as absurd with the ocean so close at hand. In decor and menu the more up-scale restaurants are trying to attract tourists with fastidious tastes.

Ocracoke's real estate boom has been a mixed blessing. As it boosted land values by 10 to 14 per cent a year it brought many of the islanders a golden nest-egg. Property prices rose anywhere from 100 to 1,600 percent in eight years. Ocracokers willing to sell their land and houses could make a killing. But for the vast majority of islanders who want to stay, the bad news is the resulting rise in property taxes. Alton Ballance, Ocracoke's young and able county commissioner, says that the latest official revaluation for county tax purposes has raised village property values by an average of 300 per cent. He contrasts this with an average rise of only 30 per cent on the mainland. As a result, Ocracokers are finding themselves saddled with much bigger tax increases than other residents of the county to which the island belongs. They naturally see this as unfair and it reinforces their longstanding complaint that Ocracoke is "the paymaster of Hyde County." This is true; despite its tiny year-round population Ocracoke is the county's largest single source of revenue.

The entire mainland population of Hyde County actually declined from 5,215 in 1980 to 4,698 in 1990. Yet Ocracoke's grew from 658 to 713 in the same decade. Dependent on farming and forestry, Hyde County is poor and undeveloped. Its income per capita is less than half the national average. Neither Swan Quarter, the county seat, nor any other township in the county (including Ocracoke) is incorporated.

When asked to pay up to ten times as big a tax increase as their mainland cousins, Ocracokers feel aggrieved. In particular, many elderly islanders living on fixed incomes find it hard to meet new property tax rates that may double or triple from one year to the next. But Ballance's efforts to obtain relief for his island constituents have been unavailing. North Carolina state law requires that everyone in the county be assessed at the same tax rate and that property be valued at whatever a willing buyer and seller would accept as a fair price. So there can be no special concessions for Ocracokers, even in hardship cases. And the fact is that Ocracoke property taxes are still reasonable by national standards.

So far there has been little sign of an exodus of Ocracokers unable or unwilling to meet their soaring tax bills. But the social impact of this trend worries many islanders. Newlyweds cannot afford a place to live unless their parents give them a plot of land. The same, of course, is true of many young couples confronting real estate costs on the mainland. But on Ocracoke, with its long tradition as a settled, cohesive community, it is particularly sad to see old family properties being sold off and split up into small lots.

This in turn raises the vexing question of zoning and

planning controls. Independent Ocracokers resented outside authority and long resisted any such regulations restricting their independence. They wanted nobody to tell them what they were to do with their property. A far-reaching zoning ordinance, drawn up by mainland consultants, was literally shouted down when presented at a town meeting in the early 1980s. Islanders protested that it would infringe on their inalienable right to store crab pots and car bodies in their front yards, erect outbuildings on their lots, and keep chickens and horses. One participant recalls: "It got so hot at those meetings, with everyone screaming, that eventually it was all thrown out. The atmosphere was such that nobody could sit down and consider rationally what Ocracoke was going to be like."

But gradually people realized that some curbs on development were essential if the village was to preserve any semblance of its existing character. The catalyst that caused this reaction was the Anchorage Inn, the four-story brick motel on the harborfront that clashes with the island's long-established architectural style. Nobody could fairly accuse the Anchorage's builder of breaking any laws. For at the time Scott Cottrell got his building license there were virtually no regulations governing such planning matters as height and setback from property lines. But the former Florida businessman had flouted the island's unwritten rules, and thereby provoked a storm.

Alton Ballance went to work marshaling support for a much milder measure than the one that had been rejected. He avoided using the emotive word "zoning." An islander born and bred, Ballance knew what Ocracokers would accept. And he persuaded a majority to back an "Ocracoke Village Development Ordinance" which would effectively stop future Anchorage Inns from being built. Among other things, it restricts buildings to a maximum height of 35 feet and requires them to be set back from property lines at various distances depending on the size of the construction. It also lays down minimum requirements for parking spaces beside motels and restaurants and limits the size and height of signs. A key provision is designed to ensure that the island's health is not endangered by inadequate septic fields, since Ocracoke has no central sewage plant. After much discussion the islanders informally accepted the proposals, which were finally adopted by the five Hyde County commissioners in April, 1986.

The ordinance was a significant first step, but much remains to be done in this unincorporated township, notably in the areas of health, roads, education, and recreation. At the time of writing the island has no resident doctor or dentist, although a physician comes to the island health center once a week from Hatteras. A resident physician's assistant provides skilled out-patient care and keeps essential drugs in stock. However, since the community has no hospital or nursing home, the seriously ill must be flown to the mainland in a helicopter summoned by the volunteer rescue squad.

Defenders of this system claim that the helicopter often can get a patient to hospital faster than an ambulance contending with the clogged streets of New York City. But in stormy weather flights may be grounded and a few of the older islanders, especially those with chronic ailments, have moved to the mainland to be closer to the care they need. Clearly it would be good if Ocracoke could again entice a doctor to reside full-time on the island, as in the past. But the village is too small to offer a physician as lucrative a practice as most mainland communities. And it looks as though Ocracokers will still have to go "up the beach" to the bigger population centers on the Outer Banks whenever they need a dentist or a veterinarian.

Something also will have to be done about sewage if the island's permanent population grows much more. The problem, according to health authorities, is that there is no place in the village suitable for septic tank installation without additional sand being brought in to raise the site above the water table. Since appropriate sand for drain fields is not available in the village, developers must buy it elsewhere and ship it in if they are to satisfy the County Sanitarian's requirements for septic tank permits. This is a hindrance to new development and a spur to redevelopment of existing sites. On the other hand, studies suggest that building a central sewage and waste water treatment plant would be ruinously expensive for Ocracoke's present year-round community. This option, therefore, does not seem realistic. So it looks as if the present septic tank system will continue for the foreseeable future. It will need careful watching — otherwise the island will literally begin to stink in the summer season when the population mounts fivefold to 3,500 persons. Fortunately Ocracoke so far has been spared one bane of other communities: garbage disposal problems. It has no landfill and no incinerator. A local truck simply collects trash twice a week — more often in summer — and takes it on the ferry to the mainland for disposal.

Many of the village roads are in sad shape. While it would be a mistake to pave picturesque Howard Street, many of the sandy roads in the newer sections of the village are potholed washboards that fill with deep puddles every time there is a rainstorm. The three bridges in the Oyster Creek district have deteriorated so far that they are dangerous.

Ocracoke's tiny school needs more staff and facilities. It does a creditable job giving its 90-odd students an education from kindergarten through high school, and because of its smallness it can give pupils close individual attention. It has one of the highest teacher-student ratios — one to twelve — of any school in the land. It tries to expand its limited curriculum by using an experimental television link with mainland schools that offer a wider range of courses. But Ernest Cutler, its former principal, has said that it needs more teachers and support staff. The school is well supplied with computers but it lacks laboratory equipment for science teaching. And since classrooms are separated only by partitions open at the top, students in each room are disturbed by the class next door.

One way of improving the island's recreational facilities — now basically limited to the school gym — would be to provide public access to the waterfront at Silver Lake. But one town meeting on this subject drew only 14 participants of whom just four were native Ocracokers. All agreed in principle that steps should be taken to curb waterfront development. But Alton Ballance warned that if people were forced to sell land to provide public access this could "tear the place apart." Ocracoke was a very complex place, he emphasized, doubtless recalling the furor over zoning. He suggested that rather than ask the county commissioners to order compulsory purchase, it would be better for somebody on the island to lead a grassroots movement. Such a campaign is more likely to be led by a mainland immigrant than a native. For with the exception of Ballance, outsiders generally play a more active role than Ocracokers in civic affairs.

In summary, then, Ocracoke is an island in transition. It remains refreshingly unspoiled, thanks to its relative isolation and the fact that the National Park Service holds sway over most of its 5,535 acres. It has been changing fairly slowly, preserving much of its identity in the process. But the reality is that Ocracoke remains at risk because of rising sea levels and economic pressures. Long before Ocracoke is covered by surging seawater — if that is indeed its fate — the island will be swamped by outside money. The danger is that the traditional "Ocockers" will be displaced by newcomers because they can no longer afford to stay. If that happens, America will have lost a small but priceless part of its maritime heritage. Ocracoke would then be no different from any other beach resort — and that would be a tragedy.

Chapter 2

Blackbeard and Blockades

Ocracoke's continuously recorded history begins, as perhaps all the best island narratives should, with a rollicking party. Hosted by Blackbeard for his fellow pirates, it lasted for several days as the buccaneers quaffed rum and barbecued livestock. Given Blackbeard's lusty nature, he and his corsairs probably engaged in an orgy of wenching. The carousing, held in 1718 on Ocracoke's southern sandflats near where the village stands today, came just a few weeks before Blackbeard's death. For it was on November 22 of that year that British sailors slew this formidable pirate, whose true name was Edward Teach, during a fateful encounter in Ocracoke Inlet. The hero of that bloody hand-to-hand engagement, Lieut. Robert Maynard, bore the buccaneer's head triumphantly ashore on the bowsprit of his sloop. With its monstrous coal-black beard, the gruesome trophy earned Maynard and his men their promised bounty.

Before these well-documented events, the island's tale is foggy and spiced with conjecture. Amerigo de Vespucci

Blackbeard the Pirate
Courtesy of N.C. Division of Archives and History.

probably skirted the Outer Banks during his first voyage of 1497-98 but there is no evidence that he stepped ashore. Nearly 30 years later another Italian explorer, Giovanni da Verrazano, sailed northward along the Outer Banks after making his initial landfall at Cape Fear, some 150 miles to the southwest of Ocracoke. He called the Banks "an isthmus a mile in width and about 200 long" — a description that was not far wrong. But Verrazano believed that Pamlico Sound, the 25-mile-wide lagoon beyond the sandbank, was the ocean leading to China and India. His crows-nest lookouts could not see the lowlying mainland across the Sound. So Verrazano assumed that the narrow sandbar of the Outer Banks was all that stood between him and the exotic Orient — just as Columbus supposed he had reached Asia when he sighted the West Indies.

For sixty years after Verrazano's 1524 voyage no European mariner recorded any further exploration of the Outer Banks. Occasional shipwrecks occurred, but it was not until 1584-87 that Sir Walter Raleigh's expeditions founded the ill-fated Lost Colony on Roanoke Island, some sixty miles north of Ocracoke. Just where Raleigh's pioneering sailors first rowed ashore on their initial voyage to Roanoke remains a mystery. But it was somewhere on the Outer Banks and there is an outside chance that this historic landing occurred on Ocracoke. If so, the island would have been the scene of the ceremony in which these navigators, Captains Arthur Barlowe and Philip Amadas, took possession of the area in the name of Queen Elizabeth. This was the first time England had claimed lands that now belong to the United States.

In any event, it is well established that Raleigh's second expedition anchored at Ocracoke, then called Wococan or Wokokon, on June 26, 1585. These voyagers, led by Sir Richard Grenville, used the island inlet as their base for almost a month while landing parties crossed the shallow sound in ship's boats to explore its western shore. They encountered numerous Indians on the mainland; Indians

29

whom Barlowe had warmly described in his glowing account of the previous year's voyage as "most gentle, loving, and faithful, void of all guile, and treason, and such as lived after the manner of the golden age." These Indians became somewhat less loving toward the white man after Grenville, in an act of reprisal for their alleged theft of a silver cup, burned one of their villages with its store of corn. The natives included the small Woccon or Wococon tribe from which "Wococan" — later Ocracoke — presumably took its name. But no Indians were found on Wococan island, which Barlowe described as uninhabited.

At that time Ocracoke was only eight miles long, half its present length. With constant shifting of the sands its eastern end, Hatteras Inlet, has changed location over the centuries. Indeed, for several decades Ocracoke was not an island at all, since Hatteras Inlet silted up in the mid-1700s and did not reopen in its current position until the hurricane of 1846.

The island's name, with its Indian derivation, has changed even more often than its geography. Successive mariners' charts and early documents show roughly two dozen variations, from Okok to Occrocokk, before today's spelling emerged in a State paper of 1782. One of the many engaging legends about Ocracoke is that its name derived from Blackbeard's fateful encounter with Lt. Maynard. According to this account, Blackbeard was moored in Ocracoke Inlet and awaiting dawn, when it would be safe to set sail without fear of running aground. In his impatience, he is said to have cried "O crow, cock!" However, the yarn is surely fanciful; Blackbeard was more of a warrior than a worrier and history relates that he spent most of the night before the battle swigging rum in his cabin.

Indeed, such revels were altogether in character: Blackbeard had a prodigious capacity for carousing, and nobody had ever been known to drink him under the table. His biographer, Prof. Robert E. Lee, notes that Blackbeard was reputed by his contemporaries to have been married at least 14 times and that he became "infatuated with every harbor-girl who caught his fancy." Yet according to this account, few pirates treated women and girls with greater respect.

"Blackbeard would customarily drink with many of the girls, pinch or squeeze some of them, and cheer and applaud them all during their dancing and entertainment. There were, often enough, a few who danced on top of the bar and the tables, with or without clothes. He would watch and enjoy them all," Lee writes. The swashbuckling pirate would then pick out his favorite, succumb to her charms and then "the great Blackbeard, terror of the seas, was temporarily at the mercy of his new-found love, and often actually proposed marriage." Blackbeard, however, often shared his wives — one of them a 16-year-old — with favored shipmates.

But he was also a dangerous prankster and one of his victims was Israel Hands, a fellow-pirate whose name was later used by Robert Louis Stevenson for one of the mutineers in *Treasure Island*. According to Captain Charles Johnson, author of a colorful 1724 description of the leading pirates of the day, Hands was drinking one night with Blackbeard and another man in the captain's cabin when Blackbeard drew two pistols and cocked them under the table. The third man prudently withdrew but Hands stayed put. Thereupon Teach blew out the candle and pulled both triggers. The bullet from one pistol shattered Hands' knee, maiming him for life. Blackbeard justified his unprovoked act by saying that his crew would "forget who he was" if he did not "now and then kill one of them," Johnson recounted.

In fact, nobody was in much danger of forgetting who Blackbeard was for as long as he lived. A native of Bristol, born around 1680, Edward Teach apparently stemmed from an educated and respectable family. Certainly he could read and write, and he consorted as easily with governors and merchants as with his fellow pirates. He grew up, moreover, during an age in which England's wealth had been largely derived from the depredations of such privateers and buccaneers as Francis Drake. Queen Elizabeth conferred the badge of respectability upon Drake's brand of piracy when she knighted him upon his return from his worldwide plundering. Johnson, in his *General History of the Robberies and Murders of the Most Notorious Pirates*, wrote that Teach went to the West Indies from Bristol and joined the pirates operating from the Bahamas. By 1716, having learned his trade, he commanded a sloop of his own and his terrible reputation began to spread.

A tall, strong man, he cultivated a fearsome image by allowing his braided beard to flourish and cover his whole face. Before engaging in combat he stuck smouldering hemp fuses under the brim of his black hat. Smoke from these saltpeter-dipped cords added to his dreadful appearance. He wore a long black coat over knee breeches, with a sash and belt bearing pistols, daggers, and a mighty cutlass. Johnson wrote that Blackbeard scared America "more than any comet" and that no "Fury from Hell" could look more frightful.

Seizing prize after prize, Blackbeard renamed a French vessel *Queen Anne's Revenge*, armed her with 40 guns and made her his flagship. When the British sent out a man-of-war, *H.M.S. Scarborough*, in pursuit the Royal Navy vessel found herself outgunned and was forced to break off the engagement in humiliating retreat. Panic ensued among the traders and shipowners in the defenseless province of North Carolina. They secretly appealed to Governor Alexander Spotswood of neighboring Virginia, who resolved to "put a Stop to ye further Progress of the Robberys."

After persuading his Assembly to offer substantial rewards for the capture of Teach and other pirates, Gov. Spotswood hired two shallow-draft sloops capable of operating amid the shallows of Ocracoke Inlet and manned them with crewmen from two British warships. They sailed from the James River under Lt. Maynard's command and arrived at Ocracoke on the evening of November 21, 1718. Maynard decided to await high tide early next day before attacking Blackbeard's ship, the *Adventure*, which was hidden at her customary anchorage — known to this day as Teach's Hole — at Ocracoke Inlet. Whether the pirate knew of the threat is doubtful, for the British ships kept their distance.

Teach's crew was greatly reduced; he boasted of having 40 men aboard but Johnson said the figure was no more than 25. (Gov. Spotswood put it as low as 18 in his report on the battle.) Maynard had a total of 54 sailors in his two attacking sloops, according to his own account. But Blackbeard had eight cannons while Maynard's force had nothing but small arms; an advantage that the pirate used to deadly effect when battle was joined at dawn.

Johnson's classic description of the engagement said that as Maynard approached, Blackbeard hailed him with the challenge: "Damn you for villains, who are you?" Whereupon the lieutenant, who had hoisted the Royal Navy's ensign, retorted: "You may see by our colors we are no pirates." As both men swore that they would neither seek nor give quarter, Blackbeard fired a devastating broadside which killed or wounded 29 men in Maynard's sloops. Undaunted, Maynard pressed on, ordering his men below decks while his own vessel continued to close with the enemy.

As the two boats grappled, Blackbeard saw that his attacker's deck was virtually empty. Teach's pirates first hurled bottle grenades filled with gunpowder and shrapnel aboard Maynard's sloop. Then, as Blackbeard led his 15-strong boarding party across, Maynard's hidden men emerged from the hold and "attacked the pirates with as much bravery as ever was done upon such an occasion," Johnson said. Blackbeard and Maynard fired pistols at each other, and the pirate suffered his first wound. But the injury did not prevent the two men from engaging in a cutlass duel until the lieutenant's sword broke. As Maynard stepped back to cock a pistol, Blackbeard swung at him with his cutlass. But one of Maynard's men intervened, giving Teach a "terrible wound in the neck and throat" and heading off the blow. The desperate hand-to-hand fight continued between Maynard's dozen surviving crewmen and Blackbeard's forces until the pirate chief finally fell dead. Johnson said that Teach's body suffered 25 wounds, five of them from gunshot. Legend has it that after his head was cut off, Blackbeard's massive body swam seven times around the ship before sinking.

Gov. Spotswood boasted to his masters in London that in secretly planning and carrying out his operation he hoped he had foiled the pirates' "pernicious design" of fortifying an island at Ocracoke Inlet for use as a buccaneering base. And indeed, the heyday of the pirates along the Outer Banks was past. Commerce and economic growth could resume.

It is significant that the operation was mounted by Virginia, not North Carolina. For North Carolina in those days was still very much a fledgling province, thinly-populated and weak. Its northern neighbor, by contrast, was both prosperous and populous. So concerned were the Lords Proprietors at this situation that they passed an Act in 1707 to encourage settlement in North Carolina by promising certain categories of debtors immunity from arrest for five years following their arrival in the province. Indeed, many of the early settlers seem to have been of dubious character: a missionary named John Urmston reported home to London that North Carolina was "a nest of the most notorious profligates upon earth."

In a letter to the Society for the Propagation of the Gospel dated July 7, 1711, Urmston wrote of "libertines Men & Women of loose dissolute and scandalous lives and practices." Noting the adage that England's colonies were chiefly peopled by ex-convicts, he observed that many North

Carolina settlers "after their transportation from England have been banished out of all or most of the other colonies or for fear of punishment have fled hither." North Carolina's Governor Edward Hyde ruefully acknowledged that although his province was one of the world's best countries, "the people are naturally loose and wicked obstinate and rebellious crafty and deceitful..."

Mr. Urmston and Governor Hyde were describing the mainland immigrants, who had mostly settled along the rivers running into Albemarle Sound in the northeast corner of North Carolina. But the thin sprinkling of Europeans who came to live on Ocracoke and along the rest of the Outer Banks seem to have been no paragons of virtue, either. And when it came to plundering ships, they were as rapacious as the pirates who operated from their sandbar inlets and anchorages. The difference was that instead of sailing out to seize ships at sea, they could wait for the storms to bring their prizes inshore. Once aground, such vessels were at their mercy.

On occasion the settlers would deliberately sabotage their helpless quarry to prevent its escape on the next tide. For instance, when the Royal Navy warship *H.M.S. Hardy* was driven ashore around 1700 on the sands between Roanoke and Currituck Inlets, Edward Randolph, Surveyor General of British Customs, wrote: "the Inhabitants robed [robbed] her and got some of her guns ashore and shot into her sides and disabled her from getting off." This was one of the first of many complaints that the Bankers — as the people of the Outer Banks were called — enjoyed nothing so much as looting shipwrecks. Indeed, the story goes that when Ocracokers were carrying a body to a funeral they would drop the coffin and run to the beach whenever the cry "ship ashore!" was heard.

Sometimes the allegedly "wild and ungovernable" islanders met their match, as in 1741 when some Spanish privateers took possession of Ocracoke Inlet, seized incoming vessels, killed cattle and devastated the island. It cost the province more than ten thousand pounds to send relief supplies. But nine years later the Ocracokers took their revenge on the Spaniards when the 500-ton Spanish treasure ship *Nuestra Senora de Guadelupe* was wrecked on the island with two accompanying vessels. The islanders plundered the stricken ships in total disregard of provincial authorities. Thomas Child, the North Carolina attorney-general, wrote that the incident displayed the weakness of civil power and the governor's inability to enforce order in the face of "a Villanious [sic] Confederacy" on the part of the islanders.

Whales stranded on the beach provided another treasure trove for the Bankers, who sliced them up, boiled the blubber and extracted the oil, bone, and ambergris. When they were not looting shipwrecks or beachcombing, the scattered residents of the Outer Banks were fishing, farming or hunting game and wildfowl. As contemporary records show, the Bankers kept cattle and hogs, while growing vegetables in their sandy garden plots.

By the mid-1700s the population of North Carolina as a whole topped 100,000, having doubled within two decades. According to one estimate, in 1760 the fast-growing colony contained 45,000 English, 40,000 Scots, 15,000 Germans, and 30,000 Negroes. Ocracoke joined in this expansion. Responding to the growth in trade and the importance of Ocracoke Inlet as the chief gateway to the mainland ports, the North Carolina Assembly had passed as early as 1715 the first of a series of acts encouraging the settlement and maintenance of pilots at Ocracoke. It was the task of these pilots to guide ships across the sandbar at the inlet and past the shoals of Pamlico Sound to the mainland ports of New Bern, Edenton, and Bath.

Four years later the Deputies of the Lords Proprietors gave a prominent mainland citizen named John Lovick title to Ocracoke Island, which then comprised a mere 2,110 acres.

Lovick was himself a deputy as well as being Secretary of the colony. A Welsh Quaker, son of Sir Edward Lovick of London, he was said to have settled near New Bern in 1710. The isle was acquired some years later by Richard Sanderson, who died in 1733 leaving "ye Island of Ocreecock, w'th all the Stock of Horses, Cattle, Sheep & Hoggs, thereunto belonging" to his son Richard. Then it was sold in 1759 to William Howard of North Carolina for just over one hundred pounds, a transfer which has caused conjecture ever since.

It is family lore among descendants of the Howards living on Ocracoke today that this was the same William Howard as the notorious pirate who served as Blackbeard's quartermaster and was arrested shortly before the fateful battle in Ocracoke Inlet. He was tried for piracy, convicted and sentenced to death, but was spared by royal pardon on the very eve of his execution in Williamsburg. In theory, then, he could have been the man who bought Ocracoke Island 41 years later. A Howard family historian has called this speculation "more fancy than fact," arguing that if it were true Howard would have been only 18 at the time of his trial and still younger when he was Blackbeard's quartermaster.

The debate continues, however, since others recall that many sailors went to sea as boys in the 18th century and rose to quartermaster or boatswain rank while still in their teens. Undisputed, however, is the fact that the William Howard who bought the island — former pirate or not — was the founder of a family dynasty on Ocracoke which lent its name to Howard Street and has continued ever since.

While there is no evidence that any native Indians lived on the island when it was initially granted to Lovick in 1719, we do know that an undetermined number of Indians had inhabited neighboring Hatteras Island some ten years earlier. John Lawson, surveyor-general of the Carolina colony, reported in 1709 that he had found Indians there who claimed that among their ancestors were white people who could "talk in a Book, as we [Europeans] do." In other words, they could read and write. He also discovered that some of the Hatteras Indians of his day had gray eyes, unlike other Indians.

Indeed, it was widely believed for many years that these coastal Indians traced part of their ancestry to survivors of the Lost Colony at Roanoke. This speculation originated with the famous clue left by the Lost Colonists themselves at their deserted Fort Raleigh settlement: the word "Croatoan" carved on a tree. This was their name for what later became Hatteras Island. John White, the former governor of the Lost Colony who led the relief party, wrote that he was "greatly joyed" to find this one-word message, which he took as a "certain token" of his vanished settlers having moved to the coastal island.

The debate as to whether this really happened is intriguing and persists to this day. Rival theories suggest that the settlers died at Fort Raleigh of famine or Indian conquest, or that they moved to Virginia's Dismal Swamp instead of the Outer Banks. David Stick, the well-known Outer Banks historian, reviewed the conjecture in a recent book and concluded that no one really knew what happened to the Lost Colony, "and very likely no one ever will."

Following the Assembly's 1715 law providing for harbor pilots on Ocracoke, the first settlement on the island was named Pilot Town and built on the site of the present Ocracoke Village. As commerce through the inlet continued to grow, former Governor Burrington wrote to H.M. Customs Commissioners in 1736 urging the establishment of a customs post at Ocracoke, which he lauded as "an airy and healthy place abounding with excellent Fish and wild Fowl." He noted that such a station would prevent the kind of smuggling that had recently occurred when a French ship had brought wines, brandy, tea and other contraband through the unguarded inlet for transshipment to Virginia. He wrote: "If a Port is settled on Ocacock Island a Town will soon be built which will become in a little time a place of great commerce." His words proved prophetic: Ocracoke and neighboring Portsmouth Island across the narrow inlet soon developed into thriving ports where oceangoing ships could transfer their cargoes onto shallow-draft lighters for the Pamlico Sound crossing.

In addition, the strategic significance of Ocracoke Inlet became clear long before the American Revolution. As early as 1755 Governor Arthur Dobbs reported to his masters in London that he had ordered construction of a battery and barracks on Portsmouth Island for the defense of Ocracoke inlet. At that time Portsmouth was as devoid of inhabitants as it is today, although it had been "appointed" a town by the North Carolina Assembly in 1753. Gov. Dobbs' initiative brought Portsmouth to life and a certain John Tolson reportedly bought the first of its half-acre building plots in 1756, for twenty shillings. One of its early settlers was a publican named Valentine Wade who built what was believed to be the first tavern on the Outer Banks. He was soon made a magistrate, but relieved of this post after being accused in 1759 of encouraging "disorderly persons to dance and play at cards and dice upon the Lord's Day." This was one of the rare occasions in those rough-and-tumble days upon which any islander felt moved to lodge a complaint against a fellow-citizen on moral grounds.

In his letter to London, Gov. Dobbs wrote that construction of the fort was already under way and he asked for twelve 12-pounders and eight 18-pounders to dominate the strait. By 1758 the battery, named Fort Granville, was garrisoned with more than 50 officers and men. But within four years its strength had been halved, and at the end of the French and Indian War in 1763 its funding ran out and it was closed down altogether.

Had it been maintained by the British for another dozen years and garrisoned by troops loyal to the Crown, Ocracoke's history during the Revolutionary War might have been very different. But with the fort's disappearance, American vessels were able to slip through the inlet to bring much-needed supplies to the rebel forces, much to the fury of North Carolina's colonial government of the day. Governor Josiah Martin complained bitterly in this 1778 message to Lord Germain in London:

> The contemptible Port of Ocracoke has become a great channel of supply to the Rebels while the more considerable ports of the Continent have been watched by the King's ships. They have received through the port, and continue to receive at the inlet, very considerable importation of the necessaries they most wanted for the purpose of carrying on their warfare, from the ports of France and the French West Indies. This, my lord, was reported to Com. Nothan, the Naval Commander here, who will no doubt take all proper means for shutting up that avenue of succor to the Rebels.

Indeed, it has been claimed that much of the Colonies' success during the Revolutionary War was made possible by the continued influx of munitions and other supplies through the vital strait. Ocracoke Inlet was the loophole in the British blockade through which the merchants of such North Carolina towns as Washington, New Bern, Edenton and Bath could export tobacco and other local products in return for strategic supplies: arms, ammunition and clothing. These provisions were then shipped up the Pamlico and Albemarle Sounds to South Quay; thence by wagon overland to George Washington's shivering army at Valley Forge. Pilots based at Ocracoke did their best to ensure that American vessels got through the inlet safely. When the British belatedly tried — somewhat unsuccessfully — to blockade the strait, clashes occurred as each side sought to seize the other's ships.

In one such incident, reported by the North Carolina *Gazette* on April 10, 1778, Ocracoke pilots boarded a sloop at the inlet bar and found to their surprise that she was a British privateer, "the captain of which told them, that they were come after the Frenchmen, and if they did not immediately carry him over the bar into the road where lay a French ship and a brig, with a considerable quantity of Tobacco on board, he would instantly put them to death." Thereupon the pilots had brought the British sloop in, and the intruding warship had promptly boarded the French vessels and carried them off as prizes.

"Thus has a small sloop with 4 guns and 30 men robbed this State of two fine vessels with more than 100 hogsheads of tobacco and a considerable quantity of salt," the newspaper lamented. "This surely shows the necessity of keeping some force on Ocracock Island, otherwise our trade will be annihilated."

Virginia shared North Carolina's determination to keep the inlet open, and agreed to build two large rowing galleys, named the *Caswell* and the *Washington*, to defend what Lt. Gov. John Page of Virginia called "this important pass." Oars were needed as well as sails to give the warships maneuverability. But it was not until May of 1778 that the first of these guardships, the *Caswell*, took up station at Ocracoke with a crew of 145 men reinforced by a couple of dozen Marines. Until then the key inlet remained largely unguarded, a prey to raiding and privateering by both sides. Ocracoke Island had managed early in the war to raise a "company" of armed men commanded by a Captain James Anderson, who assured North Carolina's ruling Council of Safety in July, 1776, that his independent force was up to strength and "I hope to be Capable of guarding against all Enemies who may offer to oppose us here." But Capt. Anderson evidently lacked the confidence of his political masters. By Christmas of that year the North Carolina legislature appointed a committee to investigate his conduct and his company was soon disbanded.

Ocracoke

Around this time the Ocracoke pilots were soured by a grievance: they complained in a 1773 petition to Gov. Martin that they were suffering unfair competition from "sundry negroes" who were intruding illegally on their preserve. They wrote that such outsiders were causing them "great prejudice and Injury" and appealed to the governor to deny pilot's licences henceforth to "any such free Negroe or Slave whatsoever." Gov. Martin forwarded their petition to the State Assembly, urging it to remedy their grievances. Yet the behavior of Ocracoke's pilots during the Revolutionary War was not above reproach. Captain Willis Wilson of the *Caswell* complained in a 1778 letter of their "rascality" in refusing to bring ships in through the inlet. He wrote: "it's clearly evident to me that they [the Ocracoke pilots] wish every vessel cast away, as they may plunder them."

By the time of the American Revolution, the burgeoning traffic through Ocracoke Inlet had given rise to the two biggest communities on the Outer Banks: Pilot Town at Ocracoke and the busy trading settlement at neighboring Portsmouth. A third was soon to come on Shell Castle Island, a 25-acre shoal just inside the inlet where the original Ocracoke lighthouse was built in 1798. The wooden lighthouse was not the first building on the island, for two enterprising businessmen, John Wallace of Portsmouth and John Gray Blount of Washington, had started building an entrepot trading center there in 1790. Ships coming in from the ocean could tie up at the Shell Island docks, unload their cargoes for transshipment inshore, undergo repairs and load their outbound cargoes without having to enter the shallows of Pamlico Sound.

Today no vestige remains of the once-thriving settlement on Shell Castle Island, now reduced to a mere bank of oyster shells. But in its day it boasted wharves, warehouses, several substantial residences, a tavern, a store, and a ship chandlery as well as the 54-foot lighthouse. Wallace himself lived on the island but one of his clerks complained to Blount that when he took charge of the store he failed to keep the ledgers and he would also "drink all the rum and take all the money."

Francisco de Miranda reported in 1783 that all the Ocracokers "seem very fat to me," and that they attributed their fleshiness to their steady diet of fish, oysters, and home-grown vegetables. And a dozen years later Jonathan Price, a surveyor, described Ocracoke as follows:

> Occacock was heretofore, and still retains the name of, an island. It is now a peninsula; a heap of sand having gradually filled up the space which divided it from the bank [the rest of the Outer Banks]. It continues to have its former appearance from the sea; the green trees, that cover it, strikingly distinguishing it from the sandy bank to which it has been joined. Its length is three miles, and its breadth two and one half. Small live oak and cedar grow abundantly over it, and it contains several swamps and rich marshes, which might be cultivated to great advantage; but its inhabitants, depending on another element for their support, suffer the earth to remain in its natural state. They are all pilots; and their number of head of families is about thirty. This healthy spot is in autumn the resort of many of the inhabitants of the main. One of its original proprietors, who has attained his ninetieth year, still resides on it, and does not appear to feel any of the infirmities of age.

It was not until the early 19th century that the first school was reported on the island. Another William Howard of Ocracoke sold a piece of land on February 4, 1808, to "the subscribers of the school house on Ocracock" for ten dollars.

Two years later the census showed 209 residents of Ocracoke and 387 islanders at Portsmouth. Of these, 40 were inhabitants of Shell Castle, including ten white males. But

"Governor" John Wallace died in 1810, at age 52, and the stone on his Portsmouth Island grave reads: "Shell Castle mourn! Your pride is in the dust." With this blow and the effects of storm damage, the trading settlement went into a decline that was hastened by shoaling of the channel. This same silting-up of the waters around Shell Castle also spelled the doom of the original wooden lighthouse, now a mile from the shipping channel. So in 1820 it was replaced by a lightship in the inlet. But this also proved inadequate and it was in turn succeeded by Ocracoke's present stone lighthouse, erected in 1823. Some 70 feet tall, the white cone-shaped structure is Ocracoke's true emblem. It ranks as the oldest operating lighthouse on the North Carolina coast.

Hostilities returned to Ocracoke Inlet during the War of 1812 when a fleet of nine British warships anchored off the bar and sent nineteen lighters into the Sound, each carrying an 18-pounder gun and 40 men. This sizable force promptly attacked and captured two lightly armed privateers, the *Anaconda* and the *Atlas*, but a third American vessel, a revenue cutter, made her escape and reached New Bern to raise the alarm. Panic ensued on the mainland as North Carolina's inhabitants feared — not without reason — that Admiral Cockburn planned an invasion. A committee of safety was hastily appointed, heavy cannon mounted and breastworks thrown up at New Bern.

As a "gale of patriotic ardor swept throughout the whole State," according to one account, two thousand volunteers came forward within hours to form a militia. But the threat vanished as quickly as it had appeared; after spending five days looting Ocracoke and Portsmouth of livestock, Admiral Cockburn sailed away and "troubled the State no more."

By 1842 commerce at Ocracoke was flourishing. A report by the U.S. House of Representatives' Commerce Committee found that Ocracoke Inlet was "the outlet for all the commerce of the State of North Carolina" and that 1,400 loaded vessels were passing through the strait annually. Since many vessels were often held up at the inlet by adverse winds and tides, it was not uncommon to see up to sixty ships anchored in the roads at a time, the report said. To help cope with the acute problem of sickness among these many seamen, a marine hospital was built at Portsmouth in 1846. But that was the year of the September hurricane that reopened Hatteras Inlet in its present location and also tore a new channel inlet further north that became known as Oregon Inlet.

These new openings to the sea deprived Ocracoke of its monopoly. From then on, shipping had a choice of three convenient gateways to the ports of New Bern, Washington, Plymouth, Edenton and Elizabeth City. So although few people realized it then, the inlets opened by the 1846 hurricane doomed both Ocracoke and Portsmouth as major trading centers. But for the time being both ports continued to expand. The 1850 census showed Ocracoke with 536 residents and Portsmouth with 505. Each community contained more than 100 slaves.

Soon the Civil War clouds were looming and North Carolinians had other worries than the future of Ocracoke Inlet commerce. As the war began, Gen. Walter Gwynn, a West Point graduate and distinguished engineer, built a Confederate strongpoint named Fort Morgan on Beacon Island in the inlet. He also erected two others on Hatteras Island, named Forts Hatteras and Clark. But as early as August 1861 a Federal expeditionary fleet of seven ships carrying 140 guns and 880 troops attacked the Hatteras forts. Although troops from Fort Morgan were rushed in as reinforcements it was to no avail. The Hatteras forts surrendered and Gen. Benjamin F. Butler, commander of the attacking troops, seized more than 700 prisoners. Described as a "peculiarly small-sized, squalid and sickly looking lot," they were paraded in New York as a living demonstration of the rebels' physical inferiority. If this account is to be believed,

Federal bombardment and capture of the Confederate
forts at Hatteras Inlet, Aug. 27, 1861. Courtesy U.S.
Naval Academy.

the Ocracokers' physique had changed a lot since their corpulence had so impressed Francisco de Miranda some 80 years earlier.

The captured forts came under the command of Gen. John F. Reynolds, who set about wooing the sympathy of the Outer Bankers — not without success. Samuel Ashe, the well-known North Carolina historian, wrote in 1908 that within a week of the fall of the Hatteras forts 250 persons took the oath of allegiance to the Union. He explained: "removed from elbow touch with the rest of the State, open to invasions and fearful of hostilities, many of the inhabitants thought to save themselves by submission." There is no word that the Ocracokers were any more heroic in their devotion to the Confederate cause than their fellow-islanders across Hatteras Inlet. The remaining soldiers at Fort Morgan spiked their guns as soon as they heard of the fall of the Hatteras forts and fled to the mainland.

Although Hatteras Inlet had by this time already overtaken Ocracoke as the most-frequented channel through the Banks, the Federal forces took no chances. They scuttled several stone-laden schooners in the Ocracoke waterway, blocking it for the rest of the war. Shifting sands then finished the job; Ocracoke Inlet shoaled up so much that ships hesitated to attempt the passage. Dredging was tried, but with little success and Ocracoke's prosperity began to wane.

Once their garrison had left and their inlet had been blocked, Ocracokers saw no more action throughout the Civil War. They accepted Federal occupation without apparent demur and went on with their daily lives while the carnage continued on the mainland. And when the war ended they had little difficulty adapting to black emancipation. Slaves had always been in the minority on the Outer Banks, and the white islanders had lived for decades side by side with black freedmen. So it was not difficult for the people of Ocracoke and Hatteras Islands, with their avowed sympathy for the

Union cause, to accept the liberated slaves as members of their community.

Decades of decline ensued for both Ocracoke and Portsmouth islands as more and more ships bypassed their once-busy inlet. Within a century, Portsmouth became a ghost island devoid of year-round residents. Ocracoke's population stagnated as its inhabitants struggled to make a living. With their income from entrepot trading and piloting gone, Ocracokers had to fall back on fishing. The island was too small to attract industry; and it had no deepwater harbor. There was little to do but try to raise livestock on the sandy soil and extract a living from the sea.

Fishing was not the only way of exploiting the ocean; the islanders continued their traditional occupation of beachcombing in search of material from shipwrecks. Such wrecks along the barrier islands were not confined to the infamous Diamond Shoals off Cape Hatteras. The so-called Graveyard of the Atlantic extended far along the Outer Banks and Ocracoke's 16-mile shoreline exacted its share of Nature's spoils. David Stick, in his authoritative history of shipwrecks along the Banks, lists 37 as having occurred on the beaches of Ocracoke or in Ocracoke Inlet.

One of the most disastrous was the destruction of the steamboat *Home*, 550 tons, in the violent hurricane of September 1837. Some 90 people, mostly passengers, were lost including most of the women and children. Ocracoke villagers took in the 40 survivors and next day, Stick recounts, only the boilers remained above water to mark the spot where "the finest steam packet afloat had ended her third and last voyage." In a single storm of July 1842, fourteen ships were reported aground on the Sound side of Ocracoke Island and six more were swept out to sea from the inlet and presumed lost.

Half a century later the Ocracokers allegedly failed to assist the schooner *Richard S. Spofford*, 488 tons, when she was wrecked in Ocracoke Inlet and fetched up close to the village. Without proper equipment no rescue attempt was feasible. But instead of notifying the nearest lifesaving stations, the villagers merely stood by and watched, according to an official report. The *Spofford's* eight-man crew had to struggle ashore as best they could until the Ocracoke lifesaving surfmen, finally alerted by their Portsmouth colleagues, arrived with a breeches buoy. In the end, all but one were saved. But Ocracoke's idle onlookers hardly emerged from the 1894 incident as heroes.

There was a longstanding method of dividing up the spoils when timber or other cargo from stranded ships was swept up on the beaches. Islanders would collect such flotsam in piles on the shore and mark them for identification. Then in due course an auction sale or "vendue" would be held, usually right there on the beach, by a so-called "Vendue Master." The Outer Banks had been divided into wreck districts, each with its own Vendue Master, as early as the 18th century. But the system was still employed as recently as 1928, when the schooner *George W. Truitt Jr.* was wrecked on Ocracoke with a load of lumber. Proceeds of the sale went to the owners of the cargo, or their insurers, while the islanders who had collected salvage would get their individual piles at bargain prices.

Given the frequency of shipwrecks along the Outer Banks, it is surprising that no lifesaving station was built on Ocracoke until 1883, twelve years after the U.S. Lifesaving Service was established. Its first keeper and his assistant bore traditional Ocracoke names: James W. Howard and F.O. O'Neal. Joined in September by a winter crew of six patrolmen, they went on four-hour night patrols, conducted regular boat drills, and practiced resuscitation. The lifesaving service — which merged with the Revenue Cutter Service to form the U.S. Coast Guard in 1915 — not only served seamen in distress; its modest payroll served to buoy the island's flagging economy, as does the income from the Coast Guard to this day.

Ocracoke's first lifesaving station was located beside Hatteras Inlet. One of its patrolmen made this confession in its logbook in April 1884: "On March 25 one of the crew from this station was taken very sick suddenly. I gave him from the medicine chest about an ounce of castor oil and half an ounce of whiskey. We was so far from any store that we cannot get to them. The store is about 10 miles from the station. Thinking I had the privlege [sic] so to do and forgetting to put it down in the log March 25. Please excuse my negligence." Clearly the surfman was afraid his superiors would suspect he had nabbed the whisky for other purposes.

Lifesaving service officials soon recommended that a second station be established closer to the village. "The Ocracoke Station is too far distant to admit of its being relied upon to cover ... the lower end of the island," one of them wrote to his Washington, D.C. headquarters in 1895. "There is always the possibility of a wreck occurring in that locality that might not be known for days to the crew of this Station." In addition, he stressed the difficulty of transporting boats and beach apparatus long distances on the soft sand, especially when "horses or mules might, as they often do, even for short distances, refuse to face the fury of a heavy storm." And with the unhappy memory of the *Spofford* shipwreck in mind, another lifesaving official wrote in 1896: "It is a regrettable fact ... that the inhabitants [of Ocracoke] have not shown any disposition in the past to cooperate with the Keeper of Ocracoke Station, in informing him of any wreck occurring at this point, and there is no reason to believe that they will be any more active in the future."

To meet these complaints an additional lifesaving station was built at Ocracoke Village soon after the turn of the century, and the name of the original one was changed to Hatteras Inlet. Both were succeeded by Coast Guard stations, only one of which survives today. The one next to Hatteras

Inlet was destroyed in a 1955 storm and only its pilings remain.

Hopes that Ocracoke Inlet might once again become a major thoroughfare were raised in 1893 when the U.S. Army Corps of Engineers studied the feasibility of deepening the channel. For by that time Hatteras Inlet, too, had silted up. Two years later such a dredging project was actually started, but by then it was already too late. Ships were accustomed to using inland waterways such as the Albemarle and Chesapeake Canal linking Currituck Sound with Chesapeake Bay. They saw no need to take the long way around and expose themselves to the hazards of Cape Hatteras and the ocean storms. And the eventual creation of the Intracoastal Waterway, providing a sheltered route from Chesapeake Bay to Beaufort, N.C., destroyed all prospect of reviving Ocracoke Inlet as anything more than a fishing channel.

So the island remained in the economic doldrums through the early decades of the 20th century. Few outsiders except the sportsmen who came by mail boat from the mainland to hunt and fish knew of its existence. These sportsmen, forerunners of the tourist flocks that later became the mainstay of the local economy, would generally stay a week or more. They helped the islanders eke out a living in hard times; notably during the late 1920s and the Depression years, when many Ocracokers emigrated to New Jersey, Delaware, and Pennsylvania in search of work. Most of them took jobs on dredgers and stayed away for years. But in the end the majority returned to their island birthplace.

Angry controversy surrounded the establishment of the Cape Hatteras National Seashore, which came to embrace almost the entire island. The project originated as early as 1933 with an initiative from Representative Lindsay C. Warren in Congress. During the ensuing 25 years, both Warren and his successor in the House, Herbert C. Bonner, had to fight off opposition to the plan from vested interests in

Ocracoke and elsewhere along the Outer Banks. But the two North Carolina congressmen enjoyed staunch support from R. Bruce Etheridge, the state director of conservation and development, and Conrad Wirth, director of the National Park Service. In recognition of their efforts, all four men now have Hatteras-Ocracoke ferries named after them.

Typical of the opposition was a 1950 petition to Rep. Bonner signed by 266 Hatteras residents calling the scheme "an aggression," which would kill all prospects for development and progress. Claiming to represent 98 per cent of the people, the petitioners contended that the National Seashore would weaken the tax base and "take from us lands and liberties which we and our ancestors have enjoyed since the country was founded." Rep. Bonner replied that he suspected a misunderstanding: while he had no desire to impose the project on an unwilling population, the U.S. tourist trade was the largest cash business in the world and "this park would bring in more money to the Outer Banks area than will ever get there in any other manner."

Bonner's advocacy drew a mixed response on Ocracoke, where one of the Howard family wrote to the Congressman in 1952 that two (unidentified) local land speculators had circulated an island petition opposing the plan. They were acting, the letter said, out of "pure selfishness" and Bonner should ignore the protest. And in the end all resistance was overcome. The Cape Hatteras National Seashore Recreational Area was dedicated at Bodie Island on April 24, 1958, at a ceremony attended by many state and local leaders. Prominent among the dignitaries was Paul Mellon, the banker whose Old Dominion and Avalon foundations donated $800,000 toward the project. His original offer of $618,000 had elicited matching funds from the North Carolina state government. Mr. Mellon's gift was all the more remarkable if it was true that, as Lindsay Warren wrote in 1952, the millionaire philanthropist had never visited the Outer Banks; he had only viewed them from the air.

Creation of the National Seashore meant that the whole of Ocracoke except the immediate village area became federal property, immune to development. Hunting camps and other unessential buildings outside the village confines had to be torn down. Even at the village end of the island, a 500-foot strip of ocean shoreline was vested in the Park Service. Thus the entire 16-mile Atlantic beach, with its fragile dunes and wildlife, is spared from despoliation, as is all the marshy Pamlico Sound shore outside Ocracoke Village.

Despite the preservation of Ocracoke's natural beauty, life in the village is much less rustic than it was a few generations ago. Sara Ellen Gaskill, who died recently at the age of 104, recalled that in her youth the islanders had pianos, organs, fiddles, or accordions in their homes for entertainment. They would socialize at "candy-boilings" or at rag-sewing gatherings of quiltmakers. There was no electricity and of course no telephones or television. Nor were there any paved roads, only sand tracks. Lacking a central water supply, villagers depended on wells and rainwater cisterns. The two schools, one for Pointers and the other for Creekers, were open for only three to four months of the year. Miss Sara Ellen, as she was universally known, added that she had sewn all the clothes for the five boys she raised on the island.

The Sabbath was closely observed, too. Worshipers would go to one of the two Methodist churches and even the "awfulest people on the island, sinful people, always put their nets up, hauled their boats, till Monday morning," she said in a 1974 interview.

The *Beaufort News* described Ocracoke in 1923 as "the quaintest little town in America." In purplish prose, it said the island's 800 inhabitants lived from fishing and "the figs as fine as Smyrna's which grow wild on the sand mountains in their back yards.

"The main street is a creek, the town has no streets or roads, only little footpaths running down to the beach or connecting the rear doors of one dweller with that of another ... Horses run wild outside the little town ... cattle as wild as on the pampas of Argentina rove the ocean beach to the northward." The report said that while there were no dogs, hundreds of cats roamed the island. These had been brought in to rid Ocracoke of mice, rats and snakes which had once thrived. The newspaper wrote of thousands of communally owned chickens and tame geese, brants, and ducks.

Electricity first came to Ocracoke in 1938, thanks in large measure to the efforts of a native Ocracoker named Stanley Wahab who became a successful businessman on the mainland. Dubbed "Mr. Ocracoke," Wahab also set up an ice plant and built a hotel, cinema, summer cottages, a coffee shop, and other facilities. His Wahab Industries boasted in a 1943 advertisement that Ocracoke had "the world's finest small boat harbor" and "the finest fishing, goose and duck shooting of the Atlantic coast."

Another businessman who left a visible legacy on the island was Sam Jones, a colorful millionaire who died in 1977. He is buried beside his favorite horse on a site adjoining Teach's Hole, Blackbeard's erstwhile anchorage where the pirate's home reputedly stood. Jones left his Swan Quarter birthplace at the age of 13 to make his fortune with the Berkley Machine Works and Foundry Co. of Norfolk, Va., and in the 1950s he built several houses on Ocracoke to entertain his business guests. The most notable of these are the many-gabled mansion overlooking Silver Lake that is known as Sam Jones' Castle and the Berkley Manor, now renamed the Berkley Center and run as a country inn. Both these wooden structures are topped by square towers from which to view the island and its sea approaches. Another of Jones' local buildings is Whittler's Cottage, built beside Silver Lake with a wide porch to provide a place for islanders to meet and carve duck decoys.

A *Virginian Pilot* columnist called Sam Jones "the squire of Ocracoke" and said he dressed like a ship's captain of a previous century. He wore "pleated shirts, the collar crossed underneath with a black beard of cloth like a choirboy. A ruby pin winked red in one of the buttonholes like a wild bird's eye. He was seldom outdoors without a broad planter's hat on his head. Sam was as wild and capricious as an Ocracoke pony."

But neither Stanley Wahab nor Sam Jones wrought changes on the island to compare with the impact of the Second World War, when German U-boats brought the conflict to Ocracoke's doorstep. During one terrifying month — March 1942 — these submarines torpedoed 18 ships within a 60-mile radius of Ocracoke Inlet. Islanders would climb the lighthouse or go to the beach to see columns of black smoke on the horizon. At night the sky was lit red by the glare of burning ships.

The U.S. Navy was virtually powerless; its surface fleet in the Outer Banks area consisted of only a few converted Coast Guard cutters and other small patrol craft. When freighter sinkings were frequent, these boats were almost exclusively employed in rescuing survivors, aiding stricken vessels, sinking derelict merchantmen, and escorting ships through the danger area. Neither this meager surface fleet nor the few short-range planes that operated from Elizabeth City could provide any effective answer to the U-boat menace.

Navy records show that the first torpedoing in the Fifth Naval District, which covered the Outer Banks area, occurred on January 17, 1942. In the ensuing two and one-half months 40 vessels were attacked, of which 34 totaling nearly 220,000 tons were sunk.

Yet in this same period not a single U-boat was destroyed. Only in three counter-attacks was there even hope that a submarine had been damaged. In the Navy's phrase, the U-boats were enjoying "happy hunting conditions" in which they could operate freely in Fifth Naval District waters, limited only by their supplies of fuel, food, and torpedoes.

Barracks and docks of the Ocracoke Navy Section Base
after the hurricane of September 1944.
Courtesy National Archives.

Coast Guard cutters at Ocracoke Naval base with
hurricane-damaged building in foreground,
September 1944. Courtesy National Archives.

There was, the Navy says, "no effective control of merchant ships along the East Coast, merchant convoys were not in operation nor were merchantmen regularly escorted, and many ships were running fully lighted, furnishing an easy target. Only a small proportion of the merchant ships were armed ... no fixed lane or routing was followed and ships were scattered from a few miles to 100 miles offshore."

Confronted with this grim situation, the Navy tried its best to reduce the carnage. Since most German attacks occurred during the hours of darkness, it set up "safe havens" at intervals along the coast where merchant ships could anchor overnight. One of these was needed in the Ocracoke area and since the natural inlets were too shallow for ocean shipping the Navy created an offshore anchorage behind a newly-laid minefield. The actual "safe haven" area was drawn on the charts just off Hatteras Inlet. Around it stretched a 32-mile semicircular barrier of over 2,600 mines, laid in twin overlapping crescents running outward from Ocracoke and Cape Hatteras respectively. The minelayers, which sowed the mines in late May and early June, left a clear channel near the southern end of the minefield for entry and exit.

This Hatteras minefield was secret. Merchant marine skippers were not told of its existence for fear that the enemy would find out. Hence the imperative need for naval escorts to guide the merchantmen safely through the clear channel, and for a nearby base at which to station these escort craft. This was the original reason for the Navy's decision to build a Section Base at Ocracoke's little Silver Lake harbor, which was as yet undeveloped.

Construction of the base, with its three deepwater piers and other facilities, began in June, 1942. It was located near the Coast Guard station, on the site of the present-day National Park Service visitors' center and its large nearby parking lots. But already by September, when the base was only 80 percent complete, the Hatteras minefield turned out to be a disaster.

Far from protecting allied shipping, the "safe haven" became a deathtrap. It claimed its first victim as early as June 11, four days before the minelayers had completed their task. The tanker *F.W. Abrams*, carrying 90,000 barrels of fuel oil from Aruba in the Netherlands Antilles to New York, entered the minefield safely escorted by a patrol boat and anchored overnight. But when she left at 4.15 next morning she lost sight of her escort because of zero visibility. According to Navy records, her skipper had been told to follow the naval patrol craft, but not how to proceed if he lost contact with his lead vessel. Oblivious to the danger lurking all around him, the *Abrams'* captain then set a course which carried him unwittingly through the minefield. When he struck the first mine he thought his ship had been damaged by a torpedo. He stopped engines and began drifting. Shortly afterwards the tanker struck two more mines in succession and her crew abandoned ship as she sank.

Other mishaps came in quick succession. All told, only a dozen ships ever took refuge in this supposed sanctuary from the time the mines were laid until the end of July 1942, when it was unofficially abandoned. The toll was one-sided: the minefield sank or damaged four friendly ships and a tug during that brief 10-week period without cost to the enemy. But other measures had meanwhile put the U-boats on the defensive: starting April 1 the Navy introduced convoys and combined air-surface patrols. During the ensuing three and one-half months the Germans lost two U-boats and probably a third within the Fifth Naval District. Ten other anti-submarine attacks were believed to have damaged their targets. At this rate of attrition the German navy found its operations off the Outer Banks too costly and ceased its attacks after mid-July, 1942.

When the minefield was abandoned, there was some question whether it was worth completing the still-unfinished Ocracoke Section Base. But the Navy decided to go ahead anyway, turning it into an amphibious training center

Tanker *F.W. Abrams* sinking as the first victim of
the "protective minefield" off Ocracoke in 1941.
Courtesy National Archives.

specializing in secret electronic warfare. Ostensibly it was an anti-submarine establishment, and indeed the monthly "War Diary" logs compiled by its commanding officer show that it sent its Coast Guard cutters out on anti-submarine patrols at least until late in 1943. Although they frequently dropped depth charges there is no record, however, that they ever sank a U-boat.

By all accounts, Ocracoke was not a popular assignment. It was dubbed the "Siberia of the Fifth Naval District" by the men stationed on the island. All base supplies, fuel and even drinking water had to be shipped in by landing-craft from the mainland.

There were no recreational facilities and it was hard to keep up morale. Cdr. Thomas A. Sheridan, USNR, then commanding officer of the base, reported to his superiors at Christmas, 1942, that there was "melancholy moaning" among his men which stemmed from a "deep distaste for Ocracoke." He added with a nice turn of phrase: "This sentiment seems to be universal and is due to the isolated position of the base, the poverty of entertainment of any kind, no liquor, and a lack of supply of the ladies of negotiable affections sought by sailors."

Two officers posted to Ocracoke at different stages of the Second World War endorsed this adverse verdict. Dr. William J. Morgan, now a senior naval historian, recalls: "I went there as an ensign and had just been married. Of course I couldn't take my bride and I was lonely. It was a bleak place, insufferably hot in summer without air conditioning and we were convinced that the mosquitoes were so big they could carry us off!" Both he and Capt. David A. Long, another retired officer, believed that the islanders spoke a dialect derived from Elizabethan English. They knew Ocracokers who had never been off the island — a species that no longer exists. Capt. Long speaks of eating "the best oysters I ever had" at Ocracoke, where he recalls seeing the islanders using horses wading in the water, dragging chains to dredge the bottom for the delectable shellfish.

The Navy brought more than a temporary boost to the Ocracoke economy. It left a lasting legacy in the shape of the first deepwater docks at Silver Lake, the first paved roads, and an infusion of new blood as its sailors married island women.

The road that really put Ocracoke on the tourist map, the straight highway that links the village with the Hatteras ferry terminal, was not built until 1957-58. Until then, the only way to get to the ferry was by driving along the beach. A tongue-in-cheek description of this erstwhile beach drive came in a 1925 newspaper article by Rep. Lindsay Warren, who termed it "the finest speedway in the world." He wrote that there were then a dozen Ford cars on the island, all treated on arrival with a protective coat of copper paint, and when driven to the Hatteras ferry at high tide they took the "inside route" about 200 yards from the beach. At low tide, "you ride on the floor of the Atlantic Ocean," Warren wrote in the Raleigh *News and Observer*. He added that "Nature's maintenance has proven to be far superior to man's," meaning that the early Ford automobiles, with their narrow tires and two-wheel drive, were less likely to get stuck on the wet sand left by the receding tide than on the soft and rutted track beside the dunes.

Expansion of ferry services was another key factor in Ocracoke's development. The private ferry that had crossed Hatteras Inlet before the highway was built became free when the State of North Carolina took it over in 1957. Now up to eight sizable ferries ply this route all day long in the summer season. A toll ferry opened up to Cedar Island, replacing the old mailboat that had long served Ocracoke from Core Sound. Finally in 1977 the first link between Ocracoke and Hyde County was established with a third State-supported toll ferry: to Swan Quarter, the county seat. Between them, these three ferry lines enable tourists to traverse the island as they roam the Atlantic seaboard.

Ocracoke does not flaunt its history. A single plaque by the fishing piers commemorates Blackbeard's defeat, and just a few old photographs and documents in the newly-enlarged National Park Service visitors' center give a glimpse of the island's past. But at the time of writing, Ocracoke's Historic Preservation Society is trying to raise funds to refurbish an old two-story cottage and turn it into a museum. Built nearly a century ago by David Williams, keeper of the first lifesaving station in Ocracoke Village, the building shows many signs of decay. Saved from the bulldozer when donated to the village by the owner of the adjoining Anchorage Inn, it was moved to Park Service land next to the visitors' center parking lot. If and when it is fully restored, complete with original outhouses and water cistern, it will display the islanders' traditional way of life.

Chapter 3

The Dowager

Elizabeth O'Neal Howard is Ocracoke's favorite Great Aunt. She may not quite be related to everybody, but she comes pretty close. Herself descended from the burgeoning O'Neal clan on the island, she married "into the royal family," as she puts it. Her late husband traced his proud ancestry back to William Howard, the Carolinian settler who bought the entire island in 1759. Originally, of course, the Howards stemmed from England where for centuries their name has been a synonym for nobility and stately homes.

Elizabeth Howard has all the right connections on Ocracoke, too. She reckons that with intermarriage down the ages her family ties extend to just about everyone who has been on the island for any length of time. Despite her mop of white curls it is hard to believe that she was born in 1910. Though tall and dignified, she soon puts visitors at their ease with the smile that sparkles from her kindly face. For 32 years she ran the village post office; earlier she managed her father's general store. So one way or another she has known the entire Ocracoke community for a clear half-century.

She remembers the island fondly from her childhood, when there were no paved roads or regular ferries except the mailboats that brought the wealthy duck hunters from Atlantic, N.C., to the original hotels and hunting clubs of Ocracoke. Born and raised on the island, she has seen it withstand hurricanes and the Great Depression. From her father, known to everyone as "Big Ike," she inherited her spontaneous warmth, generosity and hospitality. The only people she resents, she says, are those newcomers to the island who "try to tell me they know more about Ocracoke than I do!"

❦

When I came home from finishing high school in Craven County that was the time of the Depression. Well, you know, the Depression didn't hurt any of my relatives who were working for the Coast Guard or the Army Engineers, for that was the government. But my daddy was a merchant and it knocked the props from under us. Because nobody could come and buy a bag of flour, or frypans or sugar, unless they put it on the bill. My daddy ran a general store: you name it and he sold it. It was right on the water and he had a little house with a refrigerator for the ice. And he'd get 16 cakes of ice twice a week off of the freight boats. There were only two stores in those days.

When the Depression came he had a lot on his books. And it's like the old man up at the harbor said: he owed half the world and the other half owed him! It was hard to collect money then, because people didn't have any. And my family were always kind and good people who didn't want to tell them they couldn't have it. So as long as it lasted we let them have things. In my day, my upbringing, we [islanders] were like one big family. We did for each other. And no matter what we had, to eat or whatever, we shared it. My daddy would take everybody home with him to eat. In those days we had no restaurants on the island and if you stayed at either one of the boarding houses you had to eat at set times. But if you

65

were a traveling salesman, a fisherman or a sportsman you couldn't always eat at those hours. Sometimes, too, my daddy would bring people home to sleep if they had nowhere else to go. Of course he never asked for money.

When I was eleven somebody broke into my father's store. It was the old place built in the late 1700s or early 1800s. They broke in at the back, through the shutters that were held with iron spikes and 20-penny nails from the inside. They must have used a wrench of some kind. And they took canned food and candy, cigars and cigarettes. My daddy found out who did it, but didn't have him arrested. My daddy was a very soft-spoken man. I never heard him raise his voice or show any temperament at all. But he went to the back of the counter, pulled out a revolver and walked that boy in front of him to the end of his pier, where there was a little building where he kept his gasoline away from the store. And he opened the door and told the boy to get inside, and closed the door. And the girl that was clerking in the store and I — we were so scared we crawled under the counter and put our fingers in our ears! I don't know how long that boy stayed in that hut, nor do I know to this day what my dad said to him. All I know is that they came back up the pier together, the boy went home and my Dad came in. That boy was scared to death. And you know what? He brought everything back he'd taken and his father paid for whatever was missing. That boy left here, joined the Coast Guard and lived away the rest of his life. He never came to Ocracoke but that he'd come and see my father. Later my father got cancer and had to go to hospital for a very serious operation. I had to run the store since I was the only one left. The whole thing fell in my lap. Soon I got out of the grocery business and started selling ladies' lingerie, dresses, perfume, stuff like that, and managed somehow.

I married a Howard in 1942. His daddy had been postmaster here for 40-odd years and his mother came from Hyde County on the mainland, where she'd taught school. I guess he was the fifth generation of the Howards on Ocracoke. He was an electrician who served in the Navy through the war. After my husband's daddy retired I took the Post Office exam and made the grade. So I got the post office, first as acting postmaster, then as postmaster. And I ran it for 32 years. I'd never been to college because when it came to be my turn there was just no money.

Between the Pointers and the Creekers it's like Morehead City and Beaufort. Morehead City thinks they've got it all and Beaufort thinks *they* have! And that's how it was between Down Point and this side of the island, the Creek. When I was growing up the people Down Point didn't want to come here and live. Neither did those living here want to go Down Point. Actually I was born Up Trent, which is on the bay. So as a Trentist I'm not on either side. Down Point in those days there was Pamlico Inn, another inn called Cedar Grove and a line of cottages built along the shore by people from the mainland. Hardly any of them are still standing. They had Doxie's place — that was the dance hall — and a clam factory. And they had the only department store Ocracoke ever had. That was when I was a little girl, before I knew about Santa Claus. Every corner and space was a separate department: the shoes, the dry goods, the cooking utensils.

In the back they had a warehouse, and anything you couldn't get in another part of the store they kept in that warehouse. And it had a table with a book on it. You turned those pages and you could order whatever you wanted. Outside of the building they had a porch, like, and you had a little barber's shop built right beside it, with a little barber's pole. They also had a pier and a dock. It was competition but it didn't hurt my father or the other merchants either, because of the differences between the Pointers and the Creekers. The people on this Creek side were clannish and bought their groceries from my father and the other merchants over here. And the people living on the other side bought them from that side. I know my father had some customers from the other side, but they were friends of his, like the Styron family.

That place [pointing to an old photograph] on the other side was Aunt Winnie's. Aunt Winnie was black. She was from the slaves that were owned by the Blount family who were wealthy people that had places down here. She went by her owner's name, calling herself Blount. Hers was the only black family [that still lives] on Ocracoke. Now they call themselves Bryant. This black family, they ate with us and did just like the whites did. Only they were not allowed to go to school, which I don't think was right. We had a lady who taught them in her home. Every one of them can read and write, and know math. They know as much as I know, I guess! Other than school, they were accepted for everything except matrimony. That was never considered. But let me tell you: we had a black man's funeral. He was an Ocracoker who had moved to Philadelphia and died in the north. And they brought him home and had his funeral in the Methodist church. He had an all-white congregation with the exception of his sisters and his nieces and nephews, or whatever he had that had moved to the mainland, and all white pallbearers. I don't recall just when that was, but it's been since my husband died.

When I was a teenager I didn't want to live here. After I saw the theaters and five-and-ten cent stores, that's what I wanted! I liked the bright lights and the glitter. Now I've got the feeling that I'd rather be on Ocracoke than with my daughter around Washington, D.C. I like it better here, and I have roots here. All of my ancestors are buried here, although not all of them lived here. A lot of them died in other places.

There's just not many families on the island I'm not related to. I don't mean they're my immediate family, but I came down the same line. From the O'Neals, the Williams. But although I'm blood-related to a lot of people I don't have a first cousin on this island. I had 33 when I was born, but now I've got more cousins in New Jersey and Pennsylvania than I have here.

To be sure, there was inbreeding in time back. But there's fewer people deformed here, or not just right, than in any place of its size I've visited. (And I've not been to Europe.) Now I'm not bragging and someone may contradict me, but there's very little insanity here. I don't know that any of us are sort of over-bright. But it's like I told my daughter one day when we were going down the family line and she said: 'Mum, we're line-bred.' And I said: 'Honey, I know that. But so was the royalty in England and so were the Roosevelts. They wanted to keep the money in the family, the Roosevelts and the royalty in England. And we don't have anything to keep except deafness, which runs in our family, and dumbness!'

There's not as much visiting back and forth as in olden times. You know why? People have too many other things to do. They got television, they got to keep up with the soap operas! My father brought me up to welcome everybody, including strangers from the mainland. And I've lived that way. But I'll admit that there are people now that you'd like to know a little more about before you bring them home. Yet I'm not a highbrow and I treat everybody alike. There are some Ocracokers who want to keep the place as a small clan. But I don't resent [mainlanders] coming in here. We've got to have the people that are necessary. The ones I resent are those that ... didn't think we ever had anything before they came.

I really think there's a danger that this island could be swamped with tourists and commercial development. I don't like this one [pointing to the nearby Anchorage Inn], it takes my air. The breeze was always cool and now he's blocking it. The view as well. I don't know him [Scott Cottrell, the Anchorage developer], and frankly I don't care to. I don't say that behind his back. I'm not that type of person. I'd tell him that. I don't think he came here to live with us and enjoy what we've got. I think he came here to make money. That kind of person I don't welcome. And I don't know the lady that's built the [Pirate's Quay] hotel on the other side of the [Silver] Lake. It's so high. And there's an old lady — she's not as old as I am but she's not far from it — she's got little cabins close by. Now ... I could not move into a community and do something like that to the person living next to me. It's not being considerate. I think that sort of building ought to be stopped. And I don't think businesses ought to go up in my neighborhood. I'm sure everybody else feels the same way about it. I wouldn't want a motel or a restaurant or a liquor store to go up across the street or down the road from me. Right now, there's nothing to stop it. I don't know any reason why there couldn't be a tighter zoning ordinance except that it's always been difficult to get people here to work together.

I don't feel unhappy about the [other] motels and gift shops ... I feel that, as my daddy said, times change and you have to change with them. Some changes have been for the better. When I was a child you had to get on the bugeyes [the early Pamlico Sound freight boats] or the mailboat to get off the island. Now you've got the ferries. And a mainland doctor scolded me one time for not coming to him sooner. He said: 'You can get to a doctor just as quick from where you live as if you lived in New York City.' I'd never thought about that. You can get a plane. I've been taken away by helicopter after I was badly hurt in an automobile crash. But it could happen that a helicopter couldn't get in here. Then it's a problem. I don't feel cut off like I used to. If I want to go to a show, I can get in a car and go anywhere I want to, whenever I want to.

The electricity keeps breaking down and it gets on my nerves when I'm sitting here watching a favorite program and the lights go winkum-blinkum! But I'm not complaining. I remember when I was complaining as a young girl my father saying to me: 'Now stop worrying and stop complaining, they have earthquakes in California!' So everywhere you go you have something.

I've lived through every hurricane since 1913. I remember watching that 1913 one when I was three years old, standing at the dining room window in that old house. And I remember the 1933 one. That was pretty bad — it washed a cottage off the blocks, down where the ferry slip is today. But the real bad one in my lifetime was in 1944 — it was terrific! They called it the Great Atlantic since that was before they started calling them for women. They ought to call them for men, too!

Shipwrecks? I remember the [schooner] *Victoria* in 1925 — we used to go across there every night, to the beach. This house is built of lumber off of a wreck, the *Nomis* that broke up in the mid-1930s. I never witnessed a rescue in progress, but my husband did.

I'll tell you one thing. If I'd been born in New York City I couldn't have had any better life. Or as good.

Chapter 4

The Man Who Left the Rat-race

Alton Scarborough is one of Ocracoke's most interesting citizens: an intellectual who opted out of a prosperous mainland career as an industrial consultant to return to the island of his forebears. He wanted to escape the professional rut — to enjoy life while still young enough to make the most of it. Yet although he chose a simple, laid-back lifestyle, he and his wife Linda are actively trying to preserve the best of Ocracoke. For eight years after he chucked his mainland job, they ran a sandwich restaurant beside the highway. Then they sold out and bought a smaller, less demanding business: a summer refreshment stand that sells "slushies" and rents bicycles. With his degrees in math and physics, his experience in the Peace Corps, the foreign service, and as an industrial psychologist, Alton Scarborough must be the country's most over-qualified purveyor of soft drinks.

A jovial figure in his late forties, Alton's Ocracoke ancestry runs back through five generations. However, he was born off the island, and grew up in New Jersey where his father worked on the dredgers. Alton's accent betrays no trace of his Ocracoke descent, and by his own definition he is "neither fish nor fowl." He feels he will always rank as an outsider among the true natives. Yet he spent all his childhood vacations on Ocracoke and he always yearned to return to stay.

❧

It was a hard decision. I was in my mid-thirties, with a wife and two kids. I was working at the time as a consulting psychologist with a research and development outfit in Greensboro, North Carolina. I had an interesting job, a very lucrative job. It was the kind of job most people would have felt very comfortable with, in the sense that it had prestige and you traveled a lot. At one time I told the boss I finally wanted to take a bath with a full-sized cake of soap — I'd been staying so much in hotels and motels, traveling to London, the Continent, here, there and everywhere! It was exciting and challenging.

But I wanted to experience something else. I'd been there nine years and I'd always wanted to go sailing. I felt this was the time. You know, I'm very cynical about what a lot of people do. Most people go through life thinking that what they do is very important when in fact if half the people in the country didn't go to work tomorrow it wouldn't make a damn bit of difference. A lot of people delude themselves ... mind you, that's important for them since it keeps them working.

One of my responsibilities at the Center for Creative Leadership at Greensboro was conducting interviews with upper management people and chief executive officers. And the one strain that ran through all the many, many people I interviewed — and these were men in their late 50s and early 60s, very successful financially, prestige rising and they had everything that most people would say you'd want out of life — was that here they were at age 60 getting ready to finally achieve ... they thought they were going to get to the top of the hill and see rainbows and hear firecrackers. And when they got to the top of the hill they looked out and saw another hill.

It then dawned on me, for the second or third time in my life, that you want to do something and enjoy what you're doing and you ought to do it while you're young. So I took my decision. We sold literally everything we had: house, cars, furniture. And I bought a sailboat and we went sailing for a couple of years, until the money ran out. And the most significant thing about it is this: I thought criticism would come from my parents or my uncles or my aunts. I expected to hear from them: 'you're throwing away your career, your education.' Yet there wasn't a *peep* out of those people. As a matter of fact, just the opposite. Most of them said: 'right on!' Most of my uncles had reached their mid-60s, just retired. And they said:'I should have done the same thing when I was your age.'

The people who were most critical were my colleagues. Were they jealous? I don't want to attribute it to that. But they were very locked in, those people, in our society. Let's face it, at 35 or 40 years old, most people feel very trapped. If there's a time in your life when you're trapped, it's that age. You've got children, mortgages. It was no easier for me to extricate myself than for anyone else.

After the money ran out at the end of our sailing we came back here in the summer of '79. I just decided I didn't want to go back to a nine-to-five job. Actually it was more like an eight-in-the-morning to midnight job, seven days a week. I just didn't want to do that. I was getting older. I was afraid I'd wind up buying a weedeater, and once you get a weedeater you're really in trouble!

So I mowed lawns. My wife was a prep cook at the Pony Island. And sometime during that summer the owner of the Trolley Stop [restaurant] mentioned that he was going to be selling. And I said: 'Gee, I'd like to buy it.' In retrospect, it's an interesting thing. I grew up in a family where everybody I knew worked *for* somebody. The government or somebody. The entrepreneurial instinct certainly wasn't in me. I'd never even thought about it. I guess I'm the first person in my family ever to go into business for himself. I found it an interesting experience. It's been fun. But running a restaurant is drudgery. Like having a cow that needs milking every day.

You know, there's thousands of little stores in this world, little bars, Mom and Pop operations. You wonder how those people get along, do they make a lot of money or just a little bit? What's it like? I've come to the realization that in Ocracoke in particular, and I suspect in other areas like this, there's no money in running a small business. You make a living at it and, well, that's about it. You don't want to expand and become a McDonald's or franchise or do those kinds of things. I would hate to see McDonald's start up a franchise restaurant here. But I don't think there's any danger of that. I don't even see it down the road. Mainly because I can tell you that when I had the Trolley Stop I sold probably sixty per cent of the sandwiches sold on the island. And what I took in wouldn't pay the McDonald's franchise fee for a third of the year. The money's just not here. McDonald's just doesn't move into a community of 600 people, and even in the busiest days of summer, if they had all my business and all the other lunchtime business of all the other restaurants, it wouldn't be worth their while. We've about peaked. What's here is here. You're not going to get many more people on and off of this island.

If I had my druthers I'd try to make a whole new ball game on this island. I'd move the [Pamlico Sound] ferry landing to the other side of the village. I'd put a new road around the outside, ban all cars from the village and turn it into a little Bermuda. I guess I'd go so far as to announce publicly that from the 15th to the 30th September, or some such two-week period every year, the ferries wouldn't run. The only people who would come and go would be people who live here. No one else would be allowed on the island during that period of time. Maybe the week of the Fourth of July would be the right moment for doing that. Some people say that would kill business, but I say no; once the word got out that some strange little island was doing this, people would clamor to get here the rest of the year! Think of the networks filming the last ferry to leave and the lines waiting for the first one to come back! It would be a boon for the island; you would feel like you did when Hurricane Gloria went through and the only people that were left were those that lived here. And you could walk down to the store and see the same people and it was a kind of laid-back, mellow atmosphere. And you'd hear people say: 'Gee, why don't we do this every year — take a week off, be here by ourselves!'

But these are just fantasy things. Seriously, when people say it's clannish here I always reply: probably where you lived you visited with your neighbors, your friends or your colleagues. You played bridge, or you went out and played golf or something. There was a social whirl you were involved with. You come to Ocracoke and you don't see any of that, and you assume other people are doing it and you're being left out. But *they're* not doing it, either. People here don't visit with each other, except within the family. There's no tradition here, that I know of, with people saying: 'Let's get together for dinner on Saturday night.' People go to bed at eight o'clock, particularly the old-line Ocracoke people. The fishermen get up early to fish. It's very easy to become paranoid and think you're being left out when there isn't anything going on in the first place!

I don't think there's any animosity between the Pointers and the Creekers [the two communities on opposite sides of the harbor]. Nor do I think there are class differences or anything like that. I never heard my father or my relatives on this [Creek] side say anything negative about the people living Down Point. It was always a joking thing. But even today people on the Creek side don't tend to build a house Down Point and vice versa. In fact, I remember when a friend moved down toward the beach, to where the Variety Store stands now, my father saying: 'We'll come out and visit you some weekend!' And I can remember my grandmother leaving here and going Down Point to visit her sister for the weekend, too. So my perception of the island is pretty much the old village and it's pretty much the same today as it was then.

I speculate, trying to figure out why things happen. Today, if you go around this island you'll find that the houses Down Point are much better kept. They're painted and their fences are nicer.

Over here, the Creek side, the houses are bigger but they tend to be more dilapidated. And I've never heard anyone say this, but I think the reason is that back in the 1800s the wealthier people probably lived on this side with bigger homes and bigger families. Consequently they sent their children away to school. Like my father, who went to school in Washington, N.C., and Elizabeth Howard who also went to school on the mainland. Now, what happened to those children? Well, a lot of them stayed away, and when their parents died those houses tended to run down. There wasn't anyone to maintain them. You saw a general decay, certainly ten years ago — now it's coming back. But the people on the Creek side stayed put continuously.

Ocracoke's population hasn't changed much in 50 years. Maybe there are about 100 more today but the number of islanders who live here year-round is still probably less than 700. I think three things came together over the past 100 years to cause the demise of this area, Ocracoke and Portsmouth Islands. As the railroads came after the Civil War, goods stopped moving by sea and little places like Portsmouth died. Then there was the demise of the sailing vessel. Finally after the second world war refrigeration came into widespread use. Prior to that time, even as late as 1950, most fish that were caught here were salted. I can remember when they were selling salt mullet to the mainland. But by the early 1950s refrigeration was in such widespread use that people didn't want salt fish any more. Ocracoke was so far from the mainland, prior to the building of the road [linking the village to the Hatteras ferry], that the fresh fish market here really wasn't that good. If you go around this island and talk to men over 60, you'll find that most of them at some time in their lives went to work in Philadelphia or Wilmington, Delaware. There was nothing for them to do here in the late '20s and the Depression years. They fished, but didn't make a good living. They shot waterfowl and kept gardens, but there was no cash economy. That's what drove these men to the dredges to work, in New Jersey and other places up north. But 'home' to them was always Ocracoke. Some stayed on the boats up there but they came 'home' on a regular basis. My father's father spent 57 years in New Jersey but this was 'home' to him even though he never lived here. His name was Thaddeus Constantine Scarborough and he's buried in a tiny graveyard just behind the Park Service visitors' center. His father was not a Scarborough but Capt. James Best, who's buried next to the British cemetery. Best had a wife, but also a mistress named Scarborough, so he started the Scarborough line in a strange way!

My father, too, always considered Ocracoke home. His homing instinct was still strong when he was dying up in Jersey in hospital. The doctor said he wasn't doing well. But since he'd rallied some, my Dad said he wanted to come home. And he came home, on a Wednesday afternoon. I cooked an old drum [channel bass] for him, clam chowder and spoon bread and collard greens. And Elizabeth O'Neal Howard brought some dumplings over, things she'd made. And on Thursday all his friends looked in to see him. And he died Friday morning, in the same bed his mother had died in.

Even though the population hasn't grown much, the island is changing. First there was the building of the road to the Hatteras ferry landing (in 1957-58). Until then, the big event of the day was going to meet the mailboat from the mainland. And when you had to walk in the sand everywhere it was a different world. Up until the time the road was built nothing much had happened to the island for 40 years. There was the Island Inn that was built in 1912 or so, and the Wahab Village Hotel that is now Blackbeard's Lodge. But after the road was finished in 1957 there was a wave of low-level development. The Pony Island was the first motel to be built, then the Harborside and a couple of gift shops went up. That carried up to the late '70s, I guess.

But then came what I call the first anonymous building on the island. Up until that time everything down here was owner-operated. The reason people wanted to be in business until then was that they had an allegiance to Ocracoke. They wanted to live here and in order to do that they had to be in business. Nobody was just trying to make money. But the Anchorage Inn down here changed all that. It was the first anonymous building and I guess that bothers me more than its appearance. It's an eyesore, all right. Although it's a beautiful building, it doesn't belong where it is. It would look lovely at Myrtle Beach, I guess!

There's a difference in housing, too, that's come just in the last six months. Until then, people were buying pieces of land because they'd been coming here on vacation for years and they planned to build themselves a house for retirement. But last winter saw the beginning of speculative building for the kind of guy who comes down here, sees a $200,000 house and decides to buy it. That's an entirely different type of person.

I've met some of the people who came here to live in retirement. Most of them are fascinating, well-educated people who've done interesting things and led fascinating lives. But there's a lot who come to retire here, thinking they're going to like it, spend two winters and then move on to Florida or some place. They find there isn't the K-Mart, the bridge club and literary society ... the things they thought they would find here. But there is a hard core of maybe ten or twelve retired couples who are a bit different. You have to be fairly independent to live here; the average person who comes here after leading an active social life probably finds it pretty stifling.

I came here originally in 1940 when I was six months old. I spent every summer here all my life. It was second home to me, although I lived in Jersey and went to school there. My father always had the month of July off and we'd come here. Then I went to college in Maryland, got a degree in physics and taught for a while. I went with the Peace Corps for a couple of years as a volunteer. Then I was with the foreign service for five years. I worked in the Virgin Islands, involved in training. And I used to say that there were only two kinds of people who came to the Virgin Islands, the newly-wed and the nearly-dead! Then I went sailing for a while, then I did my graduate work in Florida, taking a degree in mathematics. I taught school again before going to the Center in Greensboro. It sounds like an awful lot for my 40-odd years! To someone born and raised here, I'm not an 'Ococker' because I wasn't born here and I didn't go to school here. Did you know that this is one of the few places in America where the high school alumni reunions can only be attended by the people who graduated? If you graduated here you can come but your husband or wife can't. That's a very clannish kind of thing and some people say it's awful. But I say no, if that's the way they want to do it, that's their business. He who has the rule, rules. I don't see anything wrong with that, and in a way I think it's kind of a nice tradition.

I can understand why some say it's very hard for young people to start out nowadays, what with soaring property taxes and insurance rates. But I don't think it's true. Maybe they're comparing with what they started with. But the world has changed in that regard. I think it's unfortunate that many people have sold off their land, their legacy. They've essentially sold their children out of the island, and that's discouraging. But in general I don't see any real drift of young people to the mainland. They're not being drawn by the bright lights. There's a sort of reverse snobbism here. I never hear anybody say: 'I wanna get out of here, I wanna go to New York City.' I think the graduates from the school here tend to do what they've always done. I think the pattern's fairly consistent over the years. Of the five or six in each graduating class, one or two go to college, one or two stay here, some go in the service. The girls sometimes marry guys in the Coast Guard.

As for me, when people ask if I feel cut off on the island from things like movies and theaters, I facetiously say that I've already been to the movies once, I've already played golf once and I've already been to the K-Mart, so I've already done everything there is to do on the mainland! Actually, I was never one to do those things like movies and theaters and concerts. When I've done them I've always enjoyed them, like when I was in London I would go to the symphony. But it's not part of my life. If I'm cut off from anything, I'm cut off from stimulating conversation. There are very few people here who can argue. I like to argue!

81

Chapter 5

The Gentle Guide

Thurston Gaskill does not look like a typical stalwart Tar Heel sportsman. Now in his late eighties, he is small (5 foot 5 inches) and slight of build. Only his sinewy wrists and hands testify to a lifetime of hunting and fishing.

He is soft-spoken and a natural gentleman with courtesy and charm. This silver-haired outdoorsman is the dean of Ocracoke's guides, a man who led duck hunts and fishing expeditions for six decades. He knows every trick of his trade: the habits and habitats of wildfowl, the telltale ripples on the ocean's surface that betray schools of fish.

Both Thurston and his wife Nora are Outer Bankers born and bred. He followed in a family tradition: his father, who owned Ocracoke's erstwhile Pamlico Inn, was also a hunting and fishing guide. Nora was born in 1899 in Buxton, just a few miles "up the beach" on neighboring Hatteras Island, the daughter of a lighthouse keeper.

The couple live quietly in a modest wooden home screened by bushes from the highway leading to Silver Lake. Like a becalmed beach after a storm, their livingroom is strewn with flotsam and jetsam from a busy life. Some of the photographs show Gaskill posing with other fishermen and proudly displaying catches nearly as big as himself. A well-used family bible graces the coffee table, religious paintings adorn the walls.

❦

Thurston: What I liked most about the life as a hunting and fishing guide was the people. To be successful as a guide you've got to be a very likable person and like people. When I was growing up on the island the hunters and fishermen came from much farther afield than just North Carolina. A lot of our hunting parties came from the North, New York, New England. Mostly wealthy people who would come for a week at a time. It wasn't worth their while to come for less because transportation in those days was so slow compared with today. Today — or at least at the time I quit — you get a lot of hunters who get in their airplanes and in a matter of two to five hours would be all the way up and down the coast.

For me, it all began when I was 13 and I woke up one morning before dawn to hear thousands of geese honking their way across the island. I decided there and then to follow in my father's footsteps and make my living as a guide. Back when my daddy had a hunting club on Beacon Island it took people almost half a week to travel back and forth from New York. They would come by train to Beaufort and then take the mailboat from Morehead City, starting at 6 a.m. and stopping at all the little places in between: Portsmouth, Hog Island, Atlantic, Davis. Later they shifted the route from Morehead City to Atlantic, after the road was built from Morehead City.

I had my own boat, which would hold half a dozen people. Fishing was seasonal: from April through November was what you might call the sport fishing part of the year. Of course there was commercial fishing that went on all winter out on the ocean. I did that, too. The fish leave the Sound, generally speaking, to go to the ocean. In order to catch them you go out on the ocean with dropnets. Haul them in again after a couple of hours, take your fish out and go and look for another school of fish. We didn't have any echo sounders in those days; just lead lines and the general alignment of the area and bottom that you knew.

Of course, you had bird signs. The gannet — a very large seabird, much bigger than the greater heron gull — would indicate to you before going into a dive whether he was going shallow or deep. This heavy, streamlined bird with his tight feathers and five- or six-foot wingspan is able to go quite deep — ten, twenty, thirty feet. The deeper he wants to go, the higher he gets up to make the dive. He feeds mostly on menhaden, trout, croaker and spot. Sometimes you'd see a slick, as we call it, on the surface of the water that would rise from fish feeding or having been attacked by larger fish or sharks. I'd go out very early in the morning and cover an area from Ocracoke Inlet eight to ten miles both north and south. There were maybe 50 or 200 boats working the area. And if somebody struck fish, of course everybody would converge. That's wintertime ocean fishing. When the fish began migrating in the spring, starting with shad in February and March, we'd be fishing in the Sound. After the shad all species of saltwater fish — trout, croaker, channel bass, flounder — would migrate into the shallow Sound to spawn.

I don't think there are more boats out today than in my youth, but the boats have gotten much larger and faster. They are more expensive and they have more gear. Years ago we had about 500 yards of net; today they might have three to five thousand. All the offshore fishing boats today, the sport fishermen as well as the commercial ones, are installing every type of electronic equipment.

The people haven't changed. As a general rule, most fishermen are very courteous. Most of the sport fishermen I knew were just the finest class of people in the country. The commercial fishermen were the same. Of course, you always had to be courteous about not getting too close to other fishermen so you got your nets mixed up. I've sometimes had to cut my own net to get it clear of a spiderweb of nets.

Back in the commercial hunting days we hunted the Canada goose and all other species of duck, geese and brant. The brant [a kind of wild goose] was one of the finest birds of my time. Wildfowl thrived on the eelgrass that grew up in waves along the low water, seeming almost like a blanket on the sea. Sometimes the growth was so thick that you'd have to stop and reverse your engine to get the grass unstuck from the propeller. But with the disappearance of the eelgrass back in the '30s the duck hunting has been gradually dying out over the years. We used to get redheads, our main diving duck, and scaup, which we called blackhead. This used to be the main winter ground for the Canada goose and brant. But only a few Canada geese come down this far today. Virginia, Maryland and Delaware are attracting 90 per cent of the Canada geese on the East Coast flyway by providing them with thousands of acres of food. So now those states are making a tremendous business of goose hunting. It's all gone from here.

When I look back, I remember the Big Freeze of 1917. You could walk on the ice of Pamlico Sound. You didn't try to walk all the way across because it was anybody's guess as to how thick it froze. I've no doubt that you can't solidly freeze a body of water as close to Ocracoke Inlet as we were located, at our hunting camp on little Beacon Island about three miles west of Ocracoke. One could look out and see not just a flat sheet of ice but real mounds where the ice had skidded on top. My father and I and our companion named Bill Williams spent 21 days at the camp. For heating we just had our regular supplies for the plain wood stove. Wood was all we'd got. We had no radios in those days so we just sat it out. We killed about 325 duck, geese and brants, and we could have killed a lot more but we got afraid we'd not be able to dispose of them. We kept those birds stored at one end of the camp where the temperature was just high enough so they would not freeze solid. Beacon Island still exists, although it's eroded considerably since that day. It's just a vacant marsh island now, and it's been taken over by the Audubon Society for a bird refuge.

The hunting club was just a simple one-story house with about four small bedrooms, you know, a sitting room and one big proper dining room. As I remember, it was a portable, sectional house that my father or some hunters had gotten shipped down. It had cooking facilities and a main person who worked as cook, housekeeper, or whatever. We did have a tornado come through there at one time — blew an end of it out but we weren't long getting it patched back together.

Hunters would take lunch out from the camp and they'd spend most of the day out in blinds: shore blinds, stake blinds or sometimes what we called a battery. This was a lay-down battery that you set down to the level of the water with pig-iron weights. It was portable — you took it to where the game was feeding at the time. It was the shape of a coffin with a deck around it. And the man who'd be lying in it would rise up and shoot. They were outlawed in 1917 or 18 because they were making it in a way too easy to get game. Then they banned baiting — putting out bait close to a flyway to attract birds flying overhead. They also banned live decoys, which we were using. These were live birds tethered to a ten-pound weight with a little strap of soft bed- ticking that went around one leg. That weight just lay on the ground. You put them among the wooden decoys, where the grounds were, in two or three feet of water. They got accustomed to it, and when they squawked their call would bring in the other birds.

We were hunting from November to April, and from April to November we were out with the fishing parties. So it was really a year-round business. My father ran the Pamlico Inn in the summer, and in winter he moved over to the Beacon

Island club. Although the inn stayed open in the winter, there was no business to speak of.

All the framing on this house came from the sailing vessel *George Truitt*, wrecked in 1928 in Ocracoke Inlet. It was picked up by me. When that ship came ashore there was thousands of pieces of timber of various sizes washed up on the beach. Well, everybody in them days, you went down there to salvage what you could. You'd pile up your pile of lumber there and put your initials on it. Then later a sale would be held. Each pile of lumber would be auctioned. The man that actually collected it had a big advantage because he got — I think — a fifty per cent rebate. So I got enough lumber to build maybe two or three houses.

We stay put in hurricanes. The house has stood up to them without damage, except to windows. Gloria didn't bother us much. Water didn't come into the house. We have a battery radio and keep stocks of food and water. I guess I've been through about a dozen storms worth noticing. Hazel in 1954 and the storm of 1944 — those ones really stand out.

Nora: We don't leave because we live here, for better or for worse. The ocean is beautiful in a hurricane. One time, when we knew it was hitting, we put all our raingear in the jeep and went down to the beach. The waves were mountain-high. It was more fun!

Thurston: Tourists have made a great change in our way of life. It's not the quiet little Ocracoke of 50 years ago. Financially, I think we're better off all along the Outer Banks. Spiritually, I think we've lost ground. Even if the tourists are the finest people on the mainland of the U.S., it seems the more people you put together the more conflict you're going to have. And it's definitely harder for young people to get started nowadays. They have to work harder and longer. People used to work at one job, now they have two or three.

Nora: The island's definitely in danger of losing its character because of the changes. The first time I came here I was
only 16 and I thought this was the most beautiful island I
had ever seen. And the people were friendly, lovely and just
as nice as they could be. And the horses ran wild all over the
island. So did the cattle. And there were little paths and little plank bridges to walk over, you know, not like the roads
are now. Everybody sitting out on the porch. Hello to you!
Hello! Hello! Everybody knew one another. I met Thurston
when I was 16, when I first came here. But I was older than
he was. He was not in my group! I later married and of course
he was married. But 36 years ago we got together. My husband had died, his wife had died. I was living on Hatteras
then, and he came over there. After a while we got married
and I came here.

Before the war there was no work here at all for the women
or the girls. They eventually would get married and have
children and make their homes while the men went away
and made a living. They'd have to go away and spend some
time of the year. And of course some could stay here and fish
and hunt. But to me, I think the tourists have been a blessing. I've liked every one of them I've ever met. I've thorough-
ly enjoyed them. I'm a bit of an invalid now because of my
back so I don't get out a lot. But the people who have come
to live here permanently, they go to church, they work in the
church, they work in the school, they're lovely, educated
people. And they have taught us a lot, I think. There are more
good people in the world than bad ones, anyway. I haven't
met any bad people. The tourists haven't tried to make fun
of us or intimidate us or anything like that.

Thurston: We've got very little room for expansion on
Ocracoke, as you can see. Which is good. Fortunately, we
don't have a bridge, which is also good. The ferry system is
so fine that it supplies our every need, night and day. And
that regulates the amount of people that can get on the is-

land. Of course we don't need any more people on the island than it can comfortably feed and sleep. You aren't going to get rich in the tourist business. You can, if you work hard, make a fair, good living.

When you come down here to Ocracoke and see all this free space, unpolluted fresh air, you can see why you wouldn't want to be stuck back in a city. I just got to where I don't leave any more than I need to. My wife and I go out most evenings and look at the sunset. I reckon we've seen more sunsets than any other couple in the United States! They are just enormous and beautiful ... the clouds are my mountains. You have to go out every night to make sure of a good sunset. Like snowflakes, no two days are alike. It's like I always say: if there were only four hours of the day I could see, I'd spend two hours at sunrise and two at sunset. That's what I've always liked so much about the hunting business: you have to get up before dawn to get your customers out to the duck blinds and you bring them back at sunset.

Every time I leave the island, when I come back I've remarked to my wife, now isn't that the most beautiful place you've ever seen? As far as I'm concerned, Ocracoke is the garden spot of the world.

Chapter 6

The Activist

George Rutledge is a tall ex-businessman who settled on Ocracoke in 1984 after a successful career as a research director for a paper company. Somewhat to his own surprise, the islanders accepted him readily, despite his mainland roots. He took to the native Ocracokers and they took to him, since he respected their traditions while taking a key role in community life. An energetic man, he was soon elected president of the Ocracoke Civic Club, and three years after his arrival the islanders voted him on to the board of the Ocracoke Sanitary District.

Rutledge took the job seriously, intent on alleviating Ocracoke's nagging water problems. He promptly visited science libraries on the mainland to study reverse osmosis, the technique used by the Ocracoke water plant to filter the supply it takes from underground. With his technical background he was well equipped to address its scientific complications, and he is rightly proud of his success in radically improving the island's water system.

Rutledge lives on a private road near the Oyster Creek district with his lively wife Betty, whose interests include archeology, birdwatching and gardening. An avid do-it-yourselfer, Rutledge has made many improvements to his house and garden. As they view waterfowl on the adjoining creek from their spacious book-lined study, the Rutledges agree that for all its drawbacks, Ocracoke is a "pretty neat place to live."

❦

George: Traditional Ocracokers are characters. They talk funny, dress weird, drink a lot, smash up their cars, drive around with bad mufflers, keep black dogs — to each his Labrador. There have been times when I've rocked on the porch at the Community Store and the Ocockers (Ocracokers) will be sitting down there telling outlanders some of the damnedest yarns I've ever heard in my life. Every one just pure fabrication! They make them up as they go along, in answer to their questions. The tourists just sit there wide-eyed! These islanders may not be well-educated, but they're shrewd as hell. They are survivors. They've had to be. They've run the island through second, third and fourth generations. And they're running it today.

The place is changing with the rising land values and the influx of outsiders. There's going to be more and more people like us, moving in and beginning to help the locals. Through no fault of theirs, they just didn't have the opportunities for schooling. It's going to become an island of people with pretty good incomes, well educated. If you come down here in the summertime, just count the airplanes out there on the strip. Insurance brokers, airline pilots, people in real estate on the mainland — they fly in here. Every one of them owns a place on the island. Half a dozen to a dozen live within a quarter of a mile of right where we're sitting.

I think the permanent population will grow regardless of what happens to the economy and by 1995 Ocracoke will be an entirely different place. But I don't think the oldtimers are going to become submerged in the flood of outsiders. There's no reason to submerge them. A lot of these people we're talking about are good friends of mine. And I got elected to this Sanitary District after I'd only been living here for three years. When I came I had two choices. You can complain about the way things are and do nothing about it. Or you can do something about it. So I went that road.

But I soon realized that the worst thing I could do was to flaunt my background, my business experience and so forth. So I didn't. There have been people who come down here and try to take over. They don't survive long here. They don't count. People say that things don't happen in Ocracoke because nobody's interested. But what they forget is that there are just X number of people — I'd say probably forty — in all of Ocracoke that do everything. It's not because the others won't do it, it's because they are getting older.

I came down here and got elected to be president of the Civic Club, which served a very definite purpose when it started because it did the functions that the county commissioner does now. Now we have a good, active county commissioner, Alton Ballance, so the things the Civic Club did are no longer needed. Although the club still exists, it's almost defunct.

Ocracoke is the largest community in Hyde County. It pays more taxes than any other place in the county. Engelhard, Swan Quarter, they don't come close. There's 5,360 souls in all of Hyde County. The county's mostly trees and water. They've had a real rough go of it. This place is the paymaster of Hyde County. That's what started all of this. Earlier, we were just kind of a lost relative, a lost colony, of Hyde County — "that goddamned island," as they referred to it. But Irving Garrish, the first county commissioner from here, started demanding that Ocracoke should have more say-so about what happens to Hyde County. Then Alton [Ballance] extended it. But Ocracoke is still really an entity unto itself. We are really so far, time-wise, from any government that we have to run a lot of services ourselves.

As the place keeps growing towards 1,000 year-round population, the school's got to get better, transportation's got to get better, water's got to stay up there, something drastic's got to be done about the health center. What we're going to do about sewage I don't know. Sewage must depend upon very rigorous enforcement of the septic tank rules. It used to be that you had a 50- by 50-foot house and a 25-foot area for the septic field. That's not working. Now we've got a regulation that you've got to be able to put in two septic fields on the same plot before you're entitled to build on it.

Betty: Unless they can do something serious about stabilizing these soaring land values and property taxes there's going to be a real standoff at some point. Because the fisherman's income hasn't gone up one penny. And their homesteads are being taxed out from under them. What they will do to hang on, or whether in desperation they will sell for whatever they can get for the land and do something else, we don't know. It's real serious.

George: Yes, there'll be land sold off to survive. But the people on fixed incomes, the older people, are going to die. And their sons and daughters, and their grandsons and granddaughters, there's still enough here for them, and they are making it now. You talk to Craig Garrish (the builder) or any of them, they're all talking about building their new house. I think this business about their being wiped out, I don't think it's going to happen. I think they're just too damned shrewd. They've got a lot of money, but they just don't show it. I don't think it's any harder for the young people starting out than it was for us, when we started out.

Betty: We have this to think about, though, if we were honest. We had extraordinary opportunities when there were all those cheap postwar government loans. You could go out and buy a house with nothing down. Down here, these poor kids can't touch these lots 'cos they start at $35,000. I'm not saying it's going to be a disaster, but I do think we're going to see quite a difference in what people do for a living. Because with fishing becoming almost non-profitable, they're going to have to find something else to do besides just being a scalloper, or whatever it is.

George: I think tourism's going to carry it. And like I said I think the Ocracokers will not be submerged and the young ones will make it. I think the traditional population will remain strong even as the new blood comes in from outside. The longer you come down here and the more you get to know these people, the more like them you become, because you don't resent it or resist it. You get to be one of them. It's fun. I have an absolutely delightful time here. It's a blast!

I really don't work at it. I'm not a kind of "sell me" type. I never was. One reason I'm glad to talk to you is to get across the message — you apparently feel as I do that this is a pretty neat place to live — that you're going to have to accept that you're going to live like an Ocracoker. Sometimes you're going to have to put up with no power, there isn't any sewage, hospitalization is minimal. Prices are high, choice is limited in the shops. You have to go up to Nags Head, 70 miles, if you really want to shop. It's kinda tough down here in hurricanes, we have a few bad days in the wintertime and it's murder in July and August when all the outlanders are here. But most of the time it's a pretty damn nice place to live.

It's going to be more like Martha's Vineyard or Nantucket than, say, Myrtle Beach [South Carolina]. But I don't think it's going to attract the chic and the jetsetters. You've got to be a little bit different to come down here.

94

Chapter 7

The Controversial Developer

When Scott Cottrell constructed his imposing Anchorage Inn overlooking the tiny harbor, his act of bravado hit the island like an ocean squall. Until then, few Ocracokers had felt a need for building restrictions. But Cottrell, an enterprising Florida builder, shattered their complacency. He bought a corner lot in a prime location close to the fishing piers and proceeded to erect a four-story motel which many islanders and visitors see as an eyesore. For he built it of red brick, not wood, Ocracoke's traditional construction material. And by island standards it is pretentious, since it dominates the Silver Lake shoreline. Further, many Ocracokers were annoyed that Cottrell built right up to the property line on one side of his plot. What he did was perfectly legal, however, because there were no height or setback limits at the time his motel went up in the early 1980s.

Now this has changed — thanks chiefly to Cottrell. The storm over his Anchorage Inn goaded the islanders into adopting rules designed to stop such building in future. The planning ordinance they finally approved set a 35-foot height limit and forbade construction of large buildings on small lots. Cottrell himself voted for the new restraints; his Anchorage Inn was already built.

A cherubic, curly-haired businessman with a ready smile and a broad Southern accent, Cottrell is totally unrepentant. He claims that his motel and other commercial developments have helped Ocracoke's tourist trade by raising the island's accommodation standards and attracting a more demanding type of customer.

❦

If it had not been me, it would have been somebody else in here. I mean, the time had come. And they could have been a lot worse off. You know, there's always a positive benefit in a development like this, and this is a tasteful development. Our clientele on the island has gone more upscale. There's a definite change in the last six or seven years. The traveling public has come to expect a lot. When this place went up, the boys at some of the other motels used to say, 'nobody's gonna stay at the new motel, people don't want that type of thing.' But I've seen their occupancy rates fall drastically. Alex Eley, he would say, 'Scott, they always told me nobody would stay at your new place, but I drive by here every night and see where all the cars are.'

Some of my detractors say I'm not building in Ocracoke style. But I've always said that traditional Ocracoke style is falling-down junk, leaning in the wind like it's just getting ready to fall over. Well, that may be very picturesque on a postcard but if you're a tourist down here and you've just come from a nice motel up the line and you've got to stay in some of the traditional places here, you're not very impressed. You can go over to the mainland and stay in, let's say, the Cricket Inn in Greenville. It will cost you $27.88 to stay in a room that has television controlled right from the

Anchorage Inn seen across Silver Lake.

bed, wallpaper, beautiful furnishings, deep carpets, free con-
tinental breakfast, all for $27.88! And then somebody's
gonna try to tell me that they're going to come out to the
Outer Banks and pay $75 here to get into an old room with
an air conditioner that only half works and the TV's just black
and white — that they're going to be impressed? With those
kind of surroundings?

When this place went in, you've never seen such a
remodeling of every other motel on this island in your life!
They threw out all the 20-year-old carpets, the beds that
sagged like bananas, the old mattresses. They cleaned up.
You know, the traveling public today is sophisticated. They
get to stay in a lot of nice motels. And unless the island's
going to be able to provide comparable facilities, people are
gonna say, 'I'm not going back there.' You know what the
awful truth is about Ocracoke: there's a lot more people that
don't like it than do.

Believe me, a lot of people complain. They come in and say,
'We'll probably be here three days.' Then they come back in
a couple of hours and say, 'I've driven around, I've looked at
everything you told me to, the lighthouse and the British
cemetery — now what do I do?' So I think a few amenities
are necessary if you're going to compete. What you must realize is that everybody is after the tourist dollar. I mean every
state, every town. You pass through towns that are promot-
ing some of the most ridiculous things I've ever seen. Just
anything! And we've got to compete against that, so we've got
to do something. Our beach isn't enough, although it's mag-
nificent and I love it.

When I first flew over this island in 1975 I'd never heard of
Ocracoke, even though I'd been to college at Washington and
Lee. And from the air it looked like something just out of a
storybook. Very picturesque. (You couldn't see all the abandoned trucks and cars that were on the ground in those
days!) So I landed and began looking around for a piece of

property as a second home and a good investment. And I found a house on a beautiful lot on the Sound.

Five years later my neighbor, Jean Wardlow, she says, 'Scott, you should be in the gift shop business.' I said, 'Well, is there any available property? I'm always ready for anything.' And we started looking around, and found the place where the Yaupon Tree motel now is. At that time it was an ugly lot, with a hole where a burned-out restaurant had once stood and the sewage just flowed straight into the harbor. It had been sitting there unsold for two years, and it stunk. The property-owners on both sides said you couldn't get a permit to do anything with it. But I knew there was no way you could take away a man's property rights. So I bought the lot and then set about getting the permits. That was in 1980.

Then the piece of land across the street became available and finally this piece [where the Anchorage Inn now stands] was on the market, too. Well, I didn't really want to buy all three pieces of property in one year. But I thought it was a once-in-a-lifetime deal, that they would probably not be on the market again. So I bought all three. Everybody said, 'He's crazy. That fellow Cottrell doesn't know what he's doing. He's lost his mind. Can you imagine any fool coming down here and payin' 100 grand for that worthless piece of property?' But that was before I got permits for 36 motel units, two gift shops, two piers and a marina out there. And built the seawall over there. And filled out the other side of the road. After all that was done, all of a sudden $100,000 looked cheap. And I've been hard at it ever since 1980, building first the Yaupon Tree in '80, then a restaurant in '81 that's now being remodeled for the third time. Then this place (the Anchorage Inn) in '82, one of those gift shops in '83 and another one in '84. Every year, it's been something.

I'll tell you why I built this place of brick. I have a fear of all-wood structures. If one of those old motels ever catches fire, Heaven help the people that are in it. Particularly if it's in the middle of the night, which is when most of your hotel fires occur. I wanted something that not only would not burn but would survive a storm. You know, the State says this is the only building on the island that can qualify as a civil defense structure.

It cost a lot more to build in brick than wood. The people who say this place is out of character, they forget that the Bluff Shoals motel right down the street is built of brick. So is the Post Office. And they were both built by native islanders. Okay, so this place is bigger. But since we put the roof on this building we've had nothing but compliments from people on the island. A lot of the sniping comes from people who have to compete with this. I had some folks come down the Outer Banks a couple of years ago and stop in here, saying it was obviously a newer facility. And the man says, 'One thing we've learned about the Outer Banks — there are a lot of tired motels.' Although I'd never heard it put that way, it's very, very true.

There's this talk about me being an outsider who doesn't contribute to local causes or take part in the life of the island. But I live here ten months of the year and we subscribe to every fund-raising thing that goes on here. Our gift shop contributes gifts every year for prizes at the carnival and the crabfest. Now, it's true that I don't participate at any of these meetings. But why should I socialize with people who fought this project so hard and objected so strongly? You know, they tried to block it with everything they had. For instance, they called the Department of Transportation in Raleigh repeatedly, saying: 'That fellow's putting too big trucks on the ferry, they're overweight, they're going to ruin our ferry.' So the Department sends the scale people down to weigh the (building material) trucks. Found that it was legal. They called up another Highway Department and said, 'That thing's over the property line, it's out in the street.' They sent down the engineers. They got out all the old highway maps. Resurveyed everything — no problems. They called the bank that was backing me and threatened to take their money out of it if it didn't cancel the project. The bank said, 'Go ahead, we're not backing off from our support.' That's just three quick examples of the harassment I've had.

But I have a lot of friends. Most important: I would not be where I am today if I hadn't had substantial local support. It's always the opponents that are more vocal than the supporters. But you can't come in here and do this without some support from somebody, somewhere. And remember: this hotel has the only sewage treatment plant on the island. And it's well set back from the property line on three sides. Look at all the businesses and homes on this island that are sitting on either one property line or another! People here have a tendency to say, 'Don't do as I do, do as I say.' And it's like Jack Willis, one of our elder statesmen, he's always said, 'Scott, you're not doing anything here that anybody else wouldn't do if they had the property and the nerve.' So I don't have any regrets.

Now about that zoning ordinance. Back in '82 when I built this, people called over to the County Manager at Swan Quarter to complain. And the County Manager told them, 'There's nothing I can do about that — the man can build ten stories tall if he wants to. And if you don't want to see another one, you'd better vote for this zoning ordinance that's coming up next month.' And that was the year they put together the first zoning ordinance. But in spite of what the County Manager said, that ordinance failed, by a majority of three to one. I was one of the ones that voted for it — I could see that zoning was needed.

The zoning ordinance that's in place now, it lays down that you've got to have so many square feet for a house, so you can't just keep packing them in, a house in every backyard. Those days are over. The 35-foot height limit would have stopped this building. My four floors go up to 33 feet, and then there's the roof structure above that, maybe another

15-20 feet. And I would have had to contend with the new setback restrictions, but only on the one side. That's the only place I'm near the property line with this [Anchorage Inn]. But I've built some other things since the new ordinance took effect.

I'm not worried about Ocracoke losing its unspoiled character. It's totally out of the question for the chain restaurants to come here. They're required to be open 12 months of the year. That's a condition of their franchise. Like McDonald's in Nags Head. They'd love to close for a couple of months in the winter. They can't, so they operate at a loss. Can you imagine what it would be like [to run a McDonald's] on Ocracoke?

If you turn this place into Coney Island, you'll be affecting my bread and butter. I realize — I'm not stupid, maybe I'm not smart, but I'm not stupid — why people come here. It's for all those qualities of Ocracoke we like so well. So I'm going back and reworking all my property, making it look more traditional and perhaps more up-scale. Certainly trying to make it fit as well as I can. Wait till you see the Sand Fiddler restaurant! Going to be a classic, with wood siding and shingles on the front. But growth is going to be extremely difficult to come by. The only exception is private housing. You can build a house without much trouble. But there are some serious limiting factors here. I think they'll run out of land. I mean, you can't even hardly get together a one-acre lot here, much less two or three. And then there's the sewage problem — I'm not sure it will ever be confronted. I think things will rub along at pretty much the same level as today.

You know, these islanders don't have the work ethic. I was born in Missouri in 1938 and raised to be on the job at 8 oclock in the morning or whatever and to be there all day. And to be doing it tomorrow and next week and next year. Living's always been easy here. There's always been so much food available. At particular times of the year you could go out here and work three hours in the morning and run your crab pots and make a living. It used to be better than it is today. But they didn't have to meet any disciplined work schedule. They have enjoyed the freedom of kind of working when they wanted to. And that is the reason why virtually every business on this island is owned by outsiders, who have a more conventional work ethic. And if you want to be real successful you'd better work all day at it. I don't think they're lazy, the natives. I just think that living has been easy. They had worked as much as they needed to. Unfortunately, times change. Some of these traditional means of support have been eroded and they're gonna have to make some changes. You're already seeing their income level erode.

I have one son, he's 21 now. He wanted to come here and go to school, but I wouldn't let him. I said, 'This school will not adequately prepare you to deal with the business world and the real world out there.' This is a fine little school. But anybody who graduates from this school is handicapped if they're going to leave the island. If they're not going to leave the island, well, fine.

Typical Ocracoke scene with lighthouse.

Surfcaster on Ocracoke's 16-mile beach.

Fishing boat swept up against Ocracoke house by
September 1944 hurricane. Courtesy National Archives.

Coast Guard Station seen from Whittlers' Cottage

Chapter 8

The Traditional Innkeepers

L arry Williams, a burly figure, grew up on the island in the '30s and during the Second World War. He is joint owner of the Island Inn, an historic building which served in his childhood as Ocracoke's first public school. Long one of the best-known hostelries on the island, his inn boasts a good restaurant and a large motel annex, all located close to the harbor and just a short stroll from the village center. Hearty and amiable, Williams welcomes his guests with gusto. He has not spent all his life on the island; for 26 years he taught English and drama in Virginia Beach. But he was homesick and never doubted that he would eventually return to his native Ocracoke. "All the time I was away I never thought of anything else," he says.

David Esham, nine years younger, owns the Pony Island Motel that occupies a large tract beside the highway approaching the village. A stocky, handsome man with a shock of grey hair, he speaks in staccato bursts with a strong Southern accent. He took time out from repairing the underground pipes of his septic field system to be interviewed on the motel terrace overlooking the swimming pool. Although also descended from the long-established Williams clan of Ocracoke, he was not born on Ocracoke. He came to live on the island at age nine, graduated from the island school in 1959, and then went to the mainland to train and work as an accountant. He returned to Ocracoke a decade later to run the Pony Island.

Marie Eley, along with her late husband Alex, built the original Pony Island motel-restaurant and ran it for 18 years before selling out to Esham. Born on the island in 1915 as a descendant of the traditional Gaskill clan, she moved away with her parents when only six months old. Her father, like many other islanders of those days, went to the mainland to man the dredgers. But Marie returned to Ocracoke after she married Alex Eley. In the fall and early winter Alex worked as a guide, taking hunters to the blinds at daybreak in a flat-bottomed boat. While the men lay in chilly wait for Canada geese and ducks, Marie would rise at a more civilized hour to fix breakfast for her other guests. Alex died in December 1986, and is widely mourned as one of the island's most innovative and lovable citizens. Marie, a handsome woman in her 70s, remains as sharp and alert as ever.

Wayne Isbrecht, after a mere 12-year sojourn, is a comparative newcomer to Ocracoke. An erstwhile truckdriver, he sold his partnership in a sporting goods store to come to Ocracoke, rejuvenate the Sand Dollar, and run a charter fishing business. He is continually enlarging and refurbishing his Sand Dollar Motel, one of the oldest of the smaller facilities on the island. With his wife Celia he runs it as a family business and is proud that they have doubled its size since they took it on. With his long straggly hair and massive physique, Isbrecht has an engaging grin and a shrewd awareness of business trends and changing island conditions.

❦

Ocracoke

Williams: I think the biggest change on the island came with World War II. It was not just the Navy coming in but the geography of the island changed. They filled in all of the little lakes, marshes and so on. Then the Navy brought a new way of life to the girls. I'd say at least 20 of them — a big group on the island —married sailors. And the Navy built the first concrete road. It started at the harbor, went up toward Jackson Tract, and they unloaded the ammunition there and put it in those concrete bunkers you see covered with sand. Although we had a roller-skating rink here in the 30's, you couldn't go out roller-skating on sidewalks, like city people. So it was the greatest thing for us to get that concrete slab road here. That's when I learned to roller-skate. We'd hang on to the back of the [Navy]) trucks loaded with ammo, going very slowly. All the boys would hang on, one behind the other, making a chain.

Another thing that brought a big change was the water system. I think it did as much as anything for the building and bringing people in to build houses. That started about 11 years ago — until then we had all relied upon [rainwater] cisterns.

Everybody's complaining about property values going through the roof and how difficult it is for young people to set up on their own plots of land. But I think young people are better off than they were. There's building going on and fewer and fewer couples are living with their parents than there ever were before.

I don't think it's true to say that if you haven't been born and raised here you're not accepted as a true Ocracoker. We've always been used to the outside world, and we've had good experiences because the people that moved into the island were mostly liked, very much so. Of course, with so many people moving in, there's bound to be some that you don't like.

I'm glad you call me an Ocracoker and not an Ococker. There's a difference. I'm not going to tell you what it is! ... but if you insist, it's, well, we have social classes here even though we are small, and the Ocockers are the lower class. It's like the traditional split between the Pointers and the Creekers. There used to be rival stores and churches on opposite sides of the lake [harbor]. But I wouldn't say there are more Ocockers on one side than on the other!

Ten years ago there were not enough motel rooms on the island. I was calling all over the place, private homes and everything, trying to find somewhere for a person to spend the night. But in the last couple of years it's been different. I think we have enough (rooms) on the island right now. I wouldn't want more ferry services. With the summer schedule, I think it's about as much as the island can handle. We've reached a limit. And there's no danger of the big motel chains like Holiday Inns moving in.

I voted for the original zoning ordinance. But it failed to pass because it wasn't properly explained. Zoning became a dirty word. But even the substitute ordinance would have stopped places like the Anchorage and that tall condo building across the lake, had it been in effect. Personally I don't object so much to the Anchorage itself as to the space where it is. If there were just a little more land right and left ...

I don't want to see zoning — I'd rather use the word control — restricting all commercial development to one area, such as along Highway 12, for that would turn it into a sort of Strip. And we don't want Las Vegas in Ocracoke.

Esham: This is nothing like the Ocracoke I grew up in. Thirty years ago, we used to have our horse races, all the way out to the beach. We had the pony pennings and we also had two big cow pennings a year. That was fun! We had a mounted Boy Scout troop — I'm sure you heard about that. I was one of the originals, aged about 14 at the time, and I had two horses of my own. The horse roundups on the Fourth of July got all the publicity. But as youngsters we'd also ride the horses to pen the cows. Cut the cows' ears, that's how

111

they identified their owners. There were a lot more cows than horses — I don't know how many, maybe 400. Then there were probably 100 sheep and goats as well.

Another thing that was fun: we'd drive out on the mudflats in old Model A's and trucks, speed up and slam on the brakes. And people used to take the trash and dump it out — built up a lot of dunes. But I never heard of dunes being based on old vehicles abandoned on the beach.

I'm glad the Park Service has the land now. But I do remember when they took it over, how those government guys intimidated people. My grandmother and her sister owned maybe 200-300 acres, all the land from Shad Hole Creek to Hammock Creek. And I remember government people coming round and talking to them and saying how much they were going to give them for the land. I think each of them got paid something like $1,000 for 50 acres of land. It was nothing. They condemned it. You can imagine how isolated Ocracoke was then, there was no road down here, there was nothing. These guys come down here with their slick city suits and they say that this land's selling on the books for — I don't remember the figures — say, $10 an acre, and they give them maybe $40 an acre. I remember that they didn't want to sell. But they didn't have any choice. I understand Sam Jones and Stanley Wahab, the two big landowners down here in those days, they contested it. They had the nerve, they had the money, they knew what the hell was going on. Of course, they lost their land anyway, but I understand they got paid more money. It wasn't long after the Park Service came in that they made us get rid of the cows and sheep and told us we couldn't let our horses run wild any more. We had to catch them or get rid of them.

I graduated in 1959 from the island school. At that time people used to leave Ocracoke since there were no opportunities here. My father used to shrimp here but times were hard. He'd work for whatever he could get. Just about everybody who graduated from school went into the Service.

I went into the Air Force, stayed four years. When I got out there still wasn't anything to do, so I went to college. To East Carolina [University]. Majored in accounting. I went to work for an accounting firm in Raleigh for four or five years. But then I said, the hell with it, and after buying this motel came here to stay. It wasn't that I decided I wanted to run a motel. I decided that being a CPA was what I did not want to do! I just wanted to get back here — there's just something about growing up on Ocracoke.

Now I think you'll see a lot of expansion in the years ahead. I don't want to sound like there's a lot going on right now. It's more laid-back, you know. But you're getting all these recent [business investors] coming in, you know, and trying to get rich. You never know, they'll probably sell out. And they don't even take an interest in the island activities. They're just out for themselves. I think you know who I'm talking about. His talk about raising the standard of Ocracoke accommodation ... I heard one comment he made, that he gets the cream of the crop. Well, I'm sure he gets a lot of good customers. But I've expanded my place and I've had people coming in ever since Alex [Eley] had it. That's the cream of the crop!

A good 50 per cent of my customers are repeat business. Sure, every time a new motel opens up, you feel the competition. Especially in the spring and fall. But my revenues have been up every year since I've had the motel. I'm doing all right. I think more and more people want to come here — and the State has got to provide transportation to and from the island. If tourists have to wait in line [for the ferries] that's forcing someone from here to wait in line. So the State has sort of an obligation to expand the service. They did it last year by lengthening the *Pamlico* and the *Silver Lake* [two ferries providing service to the mainland across Pamlico Sound]. They cut them in half to make them longer. By doing that, they could hold an additional 75 cars. I think they're trying to step up the frequency of the Hatteras ferry, as best they can.

I know some people that used to come here ten years ago that don't come here any more, or very infrequently, because they say the place is getting spoiled. Which it is. But for every one like that there's ten more who think it's great. The beach is one thing that will remain unchanged. And that's our big drawing card. The beach will not be developed. As to the rest, I'd like to see the island stay exactly as it is, but I don't think it's going to. It's a shame that there's places — like the Anchorage and that other monstrosity that's going up there — that insist on using up every possible inch of space. If everybody built with that kind of density, we'd be floating on sewage in a very short time. Maybe the zoning ordinance will save us from that. But I think one of these days like everywheres else the water's going to be contaminated because of this growing density. I'm all right because I've got 40 rooms on three and a half acres. I have my sewage plant right here! But in some of the more densely populated parts of the village, you have septic tank problems that need to be corrected. You can smell them.

Eley: My husband used to say you had to be born here to be considered an islander, and I was! But when I was only six months old, in 1916, my parents moved away. My father was in the dredging business, like the Scarboroughs. My grandfather was from Elizabeth City, and he traded to the West Indies for a general store in Washington, North Carolina. He'd sail on a two-masted schooner, the *Cora*, taking supplies and bringing back things like raw sugar, brown sugar, rum and what-have-you. He was in charge, and he made the quickest sailing trip ever made to the West Indies and back, 21 days. He'd put in to Ocracoke, anchor overnight and stay at the inn before going on up to Washington, N.C. the next day. And that's how he met my grandmother.

She was a Gaskill, one of the many Gaskills on the island. After my father moved to Philadelphia and later New Jersey, my mother and myself would come back to Ocracoke every summer to visit my grandparents.

I married Alex Eley in Norfolk, where he was working in a storage garage. Then he took a welding course and welded during the war and went on the Texas towers. But his people came from Washington, N.C. and he always wanted to come to Ocracoke with me and build a restaurant. So we came here about 27 years ago and built the Pony Island Restaurant. Then we built nine motel units, feeling there was a lack of accommodation on the island. Then we built more and more until we got up to 30 units. Since this David Esham has had it he's built still more units.

In those days there was hunting. My husband was a guide in the winter and he had three men that helped him. The game was Canadian geese and ducks — redheads, wild mallards, black ducks. My husband would get up at crack of dawn, go to the restaurant and feed the hunters, fix their packed lunch. A lot of times I'd fix their lunch the night before so it'd be all ready. Then he'd close the restaurant and take them hunting. He'd be away by 7 o'clock in the morning. He'd take them to blinds of his own in the water. They'd go out on a little creek to the blinds, in a flat-bottomed boat. There was right much limitation. I think at that time you were allowed maybe four geese. Some pretty wealthy people came for the hunting — a lot of doctors from South Carolina. As one lot of hunters left, another lot came, so it was a very busy time for my husband and myself. It was really a year-round business. We'd close around January 15, after the hunting season, and then go home to get ready for the next year.

After the hunting season it was just mostly the natives here. The community was just starting to grow at that time. Fishing was more of a business then, with people bringing in oysters and clams as well as fish. The shrimping season kinda ended about the last of November, then they'd start up again in the spring. We didn't have that many tourists in the summer; they were different from the ones you see today. There were not too many young people like are coming now, but couples and people with small children who'd come and stay a week in our motel.

Things are changing now. More people are coming in, and I think the rest of the land that's open for development will be built upon in fairly short order. The place is growing. But I've known a lot of people who come here, settle and think it's the most wonderful place in the world. And then in two or three years they decide to sell their place and move away. Now what causes that I don't know. Of course, people like their luxuries — but we've got shopping centers at Nags Head and Manteo where a lot of Ocracokers just go for the day to do their shopping and see the bright lights. They haven't had much of that in their life, you know!

Now Ocracoke has got to grow some, because if it didn't it would be like Portsmouth Island. But I think the climbing land valuation and taxes are making it hard for people on fixed incomes. Land is very scarce and there's a lot of demand. I think the islanders are asking a little bit too much for their property, I really do. But I guess that if they think they can get it, why not?

Sure, the people who are hurting because of the high property taxes could take out an equity loan to finance a little business or make some other investment to produce an income. But they don't think that way. They're not used to borrowing money. So they say: 'I hope I have enough money to pay my taxes so I can live here.' Yet there's very little poverty on the island. I don't know anyone on this island that doesn't have enough to eat and a good warm place to stay.

You'd think that young people wouldn't want to leave the mainland. But it seems that they are moving in to Ocracoke as much as ever. I've seen them come and they don't have anything when they come here. No living, no money. And the next time you turn around they're building a house. I don't know how they do it. But I think almost anybody at this time can get work on the island if they want it. There's work in the motels and restaurants. There's the crabbing business. There are plenty of jobs in the summer. And I think we have a pretty good school. It's true that there is a lot more interchange between schools on the mainland. But if you have children and have to put them in this school, they'll get an education. Of course, it's a small school, a small community. But we have good teachers and a good principal and I would say they could make it.

There isn't any real crime. Oh, maybe there's a bit of stealing, breaking in, once in a while. I'd say that you'd better lock your doors at night. I'll go to the store and leave mine unlocked. We've had two or three drug busts on the island. This is a good place for trawlers and other boats to come and unload it. Not everybody knows about it — they don't broadcast it when they find drugs on a boat. But it gets out.

I don't see any drastic changes coming on the island. There'll be more tourists and more people living here year-round. But I think the natives will still set the tone. Some of them have moved away and come back, and are running little businesses. Like Mr Scarborough, who [owned] the Trolley Stop. My husband built that after we sold the Pony Island and operated it for a while before we sold it to Mr Scarborough. You can't push the majority of these islanders. They will accept somebody if he's not aggressive and pushy. Most of them like to sort of stand back till they see that you're all right. My husband played a big part in the community and helped a lot of people on the island. But he was not a native. The islanders are an individualistic lot who are reluctant to get involved in civic affairs. We were for the zoning plan that was defeated in 1981. I think a lot of the natives were sorry afterwards that they didn't go for it, because it would have headed off the Anchorage and the condominium.

Ocracoke

Isbrecht: I picked Ocracoke because of its remoteness and its way of life rather than from a purely business standpoint. I realized that I could have made more money someplace else, such as the coast of South Carolina. But I wanted to rebuild this place, which had become run-down, go charter fishing and make a living for the rest of my life. Business was secondary. Really my prime purpose was fishing. As it turned out, my business has increased, I've doubled the size of the motel and I have to devote more time now to running it. There's more competition and the potential here is very limited because of our location. But our place is a success because it's an older building. Newer motels, suffering all the growing pains, have to charge more. I'm real proud of this place now. Sixty per cent of our business is repeat business.

When I first came here, I used to say a little prayer: that I'd never take Ocracoke for granted. And the island is in turmoil today, with all the changes going on. You see, everybody that comes here to settle wants to be the last person here! I don't know what I was thinking about when I arrived — I never expected to see it develop at all. Now I feel that Ocracoke is getting in a bind. Real leisure living is kind of gone by and by. You have to be in business every day, not like the old days, with time for fishing and the seasons you could take off. Our taxes have gone up as we've been revalued. And our insurance went up 53 per cent this year after it had nearly doubled last year.

What really concerns me is the future. I don't see how it's possible for young people, even the Ocockers themselves if they can't get land from their family, to buy a piece of land and build a house, to make a living. What's going to happen to the future of Ocracoke, because everyplace needs young people? My son, he's 24, fishes for a living, but there's very few nowadays in Ocracoke who make a living entirely by fishing. They mostly fish alone and have their own small boats. Only one islander, to my knowledge, owned a trawler — the man who runs the South Point Fish Company. But he sold the trawler. There are one or two who captain trawlers for people who are away from here. Most of the young people who want to fish are forced to work for the ferry system where they have a week on and a week off. They work toward some kind of retirement [benefits] and go fishing on their week off.

I'd like to see future development geared toward more growth for young people and private homes — definitely not shopping malls and more gift shops. In the fishing season the men usually want to go to the gift shops to bring something back home. But I don't see that there's a demand for more of those shops. Nor for shopping malls or fast-food places.

I don't want to see more motels. Two years ago there was a great need for more rooms. And I think the rooms that were added to the existing motels and hotels, plus the couple of new motels that were built, have really caught up with the demand and the increased ferry system. Five years from now all the new facilities will have been used up. There are definitely more people trying to come here, but how can we bring them in? We are served by a ferry system that's pretty well extended at this point to the limit. Actually the ferries are the saving grace of this island. I'm not asking for more ferry capacity.

Now what we have to do is concentrate on attracting people that are going across the island [from one ferry to the other] to stay here. We have to provide the kind of things that interest them and make them want to stay. And what these things are, is any man's guess. Really, Ocracoke has got nothing to offer other than purity, being next to nature in a shore area. But there's a hell of a lot of people that can't be happy with that. It's not satisfying enough; it's not relaxing enough. Many, many people ask, 'If you don't fish, what do you do here?' It's a good question. Just in the last year, we now have a boat here that takes you for a ride. We have people working very hard to take people to Portsmouth Island and provide them with an interesting day. There are a lot of things we need here, but I can't think of anything that one could make an entire living out of doing. For instance, one of the things that everybody said we needed was a hardware store. Now we have one, but they're really having it tough to make it go. A boardwalk with video games would not be refused planning permission — I don't think there's that kind of distinction made. But there's just not enough people to make it go, even in the summer with all the tourists. If people want boardwalks and video games and McDonald's, let them go to Nags Head where they can have all that, rather than bring it here.

Since I've been here, the families I've had staying with me, you lose them when the children get to be about 10 or 12. Because then the parents have to begin taking the children to the boardwalks and video games and whatever young people need. But when they get to be 19 they begin to come back on their own. We've experienced this five or six times. Young adults from families that have stayed with us begin to come back, with their friends.

One big asset in Ocracoke is our harbor. It's a really nifty thing to have, it's virtually like the home plate. But it's readily seen that it's disappearing, with everybody trying to build something around it, obscuring the vision. But I'm happy that we now have the development ordinance. True, it's very, very basic. Alton Ballance drew it up and pushed it through — it needed to be done and it's turned out well. Then of course there's the beach. I used to love to say on the phone when somebody asks if my motel has a pool that there are no swimming pools on the island — we got the biggest swimming pool in the world, called the Atlantic Ocean! But now that's changed. Some of the motels have pools and I was really sad to see it happen.

This is one of the easiest places to come as a stranger and to be accepted. Without a doubt there's some animosity builds up as the local people see outsiders come here and take control. It's very, very understandable. But they're not the type of people that become vengeful. I think they're concerned about it and I think it hurts them, and they may not do much to help you, but they won't do anything to hurt you physically or anything.

Outsiders are coming in, they have the money to build the businesses. Already when I first came here some 10 years ago, there was only one motel that was owned by an islander — David Esham of the Pony Island. Otherwise they were all owned by people who had moved in. The oldtimers here do tend to be clannish. They are in many ways really worried about what's happening. They've sold off their property and now there's no way they can get it back. So they are sad about that. When the old homestead is sold away and you build a motel on that site, then things are getting pretty serious.

Crime? It's not worth speaking of, it's so minimal. We have two deputy sheriffs here, each with an unmarked car. They are around all the time. Nobody that I know bothers to lock their houses. Occasionally you'll get a rash of fishing rods being taken off parked trucks. Since I've been here, I've had easily $7,000 worth of unlocked equipment that stays on the boat, very accessible. I've never missed anything. One of my fishing rods was taken from in front of the motel, but it had been lying around for two or three days.

Public utilities are a problem. We have to deal with telephone breakdowns continually. It's a satellite phone system and of course when all your cables are underground, as they are, they get affected by flooding. It seems that most of the electric power breakdowns are happening on the other side of Hatteras Inlet. They're working on upgrading the cable that crosses the inlet.

We are open nine months a year. We're doing maybe six months' business and the other three months are just making expenses. The season here is really just beginning to expand.

Chapter 9

The Artist-Shopkeeper

Philip Howard is a man of many pursuits. Scion of Ocracoke's 230-year-old Howard dynasty, like many of today's islanders he grew up in Philadelphia, where his Ocracoke-born father had gone to work the dredgers. Phil went to Gettysburg College and then attended a seminary. But instead of entering the ministry he headed West and taught school while learning to draw and paint. For a while he lived on an Indian reservation, where he also acquired a keen interest in handicrafts. This later prompted him to set up the Village Craftsmen store on the sandy Ocracoke street that bears his family name. He calls his business a craft shop, not a gift shop, and it offers discerning buyers high-quality pottery, woodcarvings, weaving, and paintings. Much of his stock is imported from the mainland since — despite its name — the store can no longer subsist on the products of island craftsmen alone.

An engaging, affable fellow in his forties, Phil Howard is well steeped in local history, lore, and legend. He enjoys chatting with customers. Some of them come from far afield and, since one of his pastimes is teaching himself German, he practices the language on any Germans who enter his store.

His wife Julie, who also minds the store, wrote the amateur musical "Blackbeard" that Ocracoke amateurs perform weekly in the school gym during the summer tourist season.

❦

Although I've been coming to Ocracoke all my life, since 1944, I didn't grow up or go to school here. My father lived 35 years in Philadelphia and my mother's family was from Hungary. While we were in Philadelphia I didn't even think about coming to live on Ocracoke. We came because I didn't want to do what I was trained to do — be a parish pastor. Nor did I want to do what I was doing, which was teach school. I didn't have any money. I'd had no experience in running a store. But I did have some experience of drawing, craftwork and enthusiasm for the kind of things I sell.

So we moved here in 1970 and started our business in a tent we put up on a corner of my parents' Howard Street lot. We ran it for three weeks that year in the summer season. There was another craft shop at the time, run by a lady who thought we were just crazy kids! At that time we didn't have much: mostly things we had made, and they were very unsophisticated. Some pen-and-ink drawings I'd done were probably the most sophisticated things we had. They weren't mounted or framed or anything, just strung up on a clothesline with clothespins. Then we had those little lap-type looms on which you could make the woven strands that were very popular in the '60s for purse straps or woven belts. Or you could put them all together and make bags. We just sold the strips.

During the '60s I'd got very interested in craftwork when I was out in Montana and lived on an Indian reservation. They did a lot of tanning, making moccasins with the hide. It was also during the '60s when people were doing lots of crafts and needlework. But I wouldn't put myself down as one of the generation of longhairs and flower children. You'd never have identified me as a hippie, but I was sympathetic.

We collected lots of seashells on the beach at that time. There were just hundreds of shells — it was a whole lot different from what it is today. And driftwood, and we sold that. Our entire inventory — the materials we'd purchased to make the stock we sold that summer — cost us $35. If you took ten cents worth of yarn you could make a $2 belt. I think those first three weeks we made about $200. It was worth doing.

The shop gradually changed to what it is today. We ran it in a tent again for the entire summers of '71 and '72, while I taught school here. I didn't intend to teach, but the school principal came to me about a week before school started and asked me to fill a vacancy. It was quite a challenge! I taught 11th and 12th grades and I'm sure I've forgotten all the things I taught, but I know they included English, consumer math, algebra, world history, American history, PE, and biology.

We built the craft shop in the winter of '73, ready for the summer that year. By now, as you see, we have a very different kind of operation, and I believe the important thing is not so much the merchandise; we enjoy the interaction with our customers as much as anything else.

I never had a grand plan of what I was going to do and how I was going to make lots of money. That just wasn't in my mind at all. There are things that are a whole lot more important than money. What's happened here is that the enjoyment of working with customers has led to a very loyal clientele. They keep coming back and sending their friends. And the quality of the merchandise has increased, partly because our tastes and customers' tastes have changed — a natural evolution.

We try as much as we can to get things that are made on the island. But it's just a small community. We have about 100 craftspeople represented in our shop. When you think that there are 650 to 700 people who live here, and that includes everyone from infants to 100-year-olds, there's a very limited group of islanders who have the talent and the time and the interest in doing crafts. So there are very few crafts being produced on Ocracoke. There's only one producing pottery.

To be honest, I'm not sure that the Howards are the longest-established family on the island. William Howard, as you know, purchased the island in 1759. But I believe there were a few families who were living here at the time he bought the island. But the way I understand it, he then sold large portions of the land almost immediately — I think to his grown children and some other people. And I suspect that these other people may have been already living here.

I do believe William Howard was Blackbeard's quartermaster. And I don't think the argument to the contrary made by Dora Adele Padgett [the Howard family historian] makes any sense at all. She said he would have been too young. But while nobody's certain when he was born, according to all the records I've read it was very close to 1700. So he might have been as young as 14 when he joined Blackbeard's ship. But we're conditioned to think in today's terms. My grandfather was apprenticed to a butcher and left home when he was 12 years old. And that's only two generations ago. I've not checked my logbooks for the 1700s but my guess is that there were probably boys aboard ship who were six or seven or eight years old. I suspect they may have been runaway children or orphans. Someone told me that if a man wasn't a quartermaster or some comparable officer by the time he was about 18 he could probably forget ever becoming anyone important aboard ship. Life expectancy might not have been more than about 40 years at that time. Certainly someone on a pirate ship didn't live even that long.

I had an interesting conversation with a woman just this summer. She said that while Blackbeard's logbook was sketchy, the governor of Virginia had actually sent a spy aboard Blackbeard's ship. And this person had kept extensive records, mostly of William Howard's sexual exploits! And according to these records — I've no idea whether this is true — Howard claimed to have impregnated so many women during his 15 years of buccaneering that he had 400 sons! Furthermore, this spy said that all the women who got pregnant by him knew that he expected sons. So that when he would come back into port they either dressed their little girls up like boys or they borrowed their friends' male children for show because they were afraid he would kill their children if he found out they were girls.

There's no way to check this out. But one reason I found the story convincing was because she said that according to this logbook he had these great mood swings — he'd be very pleasant and nice to the women one time and the next time he'd be utterly brutal. I have relatives who demonstrate this same kind of characteristic! I suppose anybody does, but maybe not to these extremes. Anyway, that's just a side story. But it's always been a part of the family history that William Howard was the same person as the Howard who was Blackbeard's quartermaster.

People often say to me, don't let them change anything about Ocracoke! I remember Jack Willis saying one time, everybody wants to be the last person to find Ocracoke. They want it to be just like it was when they first found it. I, too. If I could choose an ideal Ocracoke, it would be the way I remember it as a child. Ocracoke already had electricity, but we didn't have indoor plumbing and the kitchen was still separated from the house. The horses still ran wild.

My house is on the Point side, down the road from the Island Inn. When we bought that piece of property in about 1970 my father's comment was that he never knew a Howard that lived Down Point. There's not much of the Pointers-Creekers rivalry left. But you know, before the harbor was dredged during the war there were lots of little creeks that ran through the marshes around the harbor. I guess the major little finger creek went down where Highway 12 is now. My Dad said that if you wanted to go from my grandparents' house on the Creek side to visit somebody Down Point, with a horse and cart, you had to go all the way down on the Creek side of that little miniature creek to the beach and cross over, I don't know how far down, and come all the way back on the other side. So it really divided the island into two communities. In the 1930s the Civilian Conservation Corps built little footbridges over those creeks so you could walk across.

It's almost inevitable that young people are going to be driven off the island by the high cost of land. Danny Garrish, now, Craig's father, he and Margaret had enough property to give each of their four children a lot. They all put houses up around Danny's house. None of the kids has enough land that they'll be able to give their children a piece of land. This means that Ocracoke will become slowly depopulated of the old families.

My property taxes are reasonable, based on the value of my property. I think my house is worth more than it's been assessed for. But I make a living from my property. Other people buying land on Ocracoke are thinking of it being an investment, with the land escalating in value and their being able to sell at a profit. That's where the big change has come in the last ten years. I moved here because we wanted to run a business and raise a family. That's why Al Scarborough came back, that's why Wayne Teeter came back, that's why David Senseney moved here. But now people are buying land on Ocracoke purely as a speculative investment. At that rate you can buy a business and not care whether you ever make a profit selling products as long as you can sell the property at a profit five years down the road. You have a whole different attitude towards the place if you think in those terms.

Ocracoke probably will become a trendy resort. People say to me, don't let it get commercialized. But what do they think I'm running? I've got a commercial business. I don't have neon lights, but it's certainly commercial. Not only is it commercial, but it's on a street that was only residential. So it's an intrusion. Everybody says, oh, but it's nice. But it's not the way Ocracoke was when I was a child. It's different because of our shop. There's more traffic down our road. I'm not saying it's bad. I'm just saying it would be a mistake for me to think that what I'm doing is not changing Ocracoke. I like to think that it's probably had some positive impact. But it does change the island and Ocracoke will never be the same as it was when I was a kid.

In the past I was rather reactionary about change. I hated to see all the changes coming, and I still feel it was all so positive and wonderful. But I know that things are going to change. I don't necessarily feel that we should waste our energy in trying to keep Ocracoke in some idealistic way what it was — sort of quaint. In a lot of ways I really enjoy changes. For instance, our next door neighbors are black. And our attitudes towards them are much better than they were when I was a kid. And as far as that's concerned I rejoice for them that Ocracoke's a different place from what it was. They didn't even go to school here. I remember their mother and father, and how their mother just basically went around begging. Aunt Winnie was Mews' and Minnie's and Jules' grandmother. She was a slave and came here after emancipation. Mews once told me she could remember her grandmother's owner.

I think Ocracoke attracts a different type of visitor because of what we don't have. We don't have a boardwalk. One of my favorite stories is about the woman who came into the shell shop and asked, 'Is there a beach here?' Well, this was an eye-opener and the shop-owner said, 'How did you get here?' She replied, 'We came from Hatteras, across the ferry.' He said, 'Well, the entire way down on the lefthand side, there's 16 miles of beach.' To which she responded: 'Oh no, I mean a real beach with boardwalks and hotdog stands!'

You can choose what kind of place Ocracoke will be if you pass zoning laws that encourage certain types of people to come. I'm concerned about questions involving class structure, because I think in those terms myself sometimes. But I'll admit that the kinds of people who come to Ocracoke and walk down Howard Street and come into our shop are an absolute delight to have in the business. I've had a couple of occasions this summer when I've given people merchandise. Because we don't take American Express and when people don't have their checkbook or Mastercard or Visa and need cash to get back to their motel or something, I've given them merchandise. A substantial lot of money: a $59 wind chime and the other was about $64. And I said, just take it and send me a check when you get home. And I'd never seen the people before, but I knew I'd get the checks, and I did. In the 18 years I've been in business we've had one check for five dollars and 12 cents that we never got paid for. And I take hundreds of checks every day.

I can talk about lots of different things with people, they're pleasant, articulate. Some of them ask a lot about Ocracoke. At the same time they're not a real cross-section of America. I don't know what we can do. I mean, if we try to encourage only one type of person to come to Ocracoke ... I think life is so much more interesting when there's different people, different ideas.

There are a lot of things Ocracoke didn't have until relatively recently. Not too long ago you couldn't buy beer or wine, let alone hard liquor. The Pelican and the Back Porch are clearly a different type of restaurant than Ocracoke used to have. Ocracoke's now got a tanning salon, fashion boutique shops. Sailboarding is a whole new industry. VCR rentals. Those kind of things are what people from off the island, or some of them, want. Things that weren't available before.

It's not nearly as true now as it used to be that you either love it [Ocracoke] or hate it. Years ago it was very true. There were people who absolutely hated it. They didn't have adequate drinking water, all they had was cistern water with frogs jumping out of it! You would turn on the ground water and it would smell funny. People would come down and rent a cottage and think, ugh, it smells funny. That's changed. We have a water system now that's typical of any water system in the country. The electric situation now is much better than it was. The campground is nowhere near as primitive as it was. It didn't even have showers when we first had the shop — just a hand pump. There were no flush toilets, just pit toilets. That was really when people said they hated it.

Another major change is the building ordinance. When I built the shop I didn't have to ask anybody for anything. All I had to do was buy the materials and build. But when I started my house I had to get the septic tank approved, and the electrics and the plumbing. When I added on to the craft shop I had to have all of the construction, the framing and plumbing and electrics and everything, approved. So I've moved from nothing to virtually everything, on the things I've done.

I think the restrictions now in place are helpful. But there's always some way to get around even the most well-intentioned, specific and detailed laws and regulations. And the more detailed you make them, the more you're interfering in people's lives. And one of the nice things about Ocracoke has always been that it's not so regulated.

Chapter 10

The Village Policeman

Every crime from rape to robbery falls into Sergeant Gene Jackson's bailiwick as Ocracoke's guardian of law and order. He is the island's senior sheriff's deputy, backed by only one assistant. His pay is meager and his hours long, particularly in the summer season when mainlanders bring drugs to Ocracoke. Even in midwinter he often has his hands full dealing with islanders who break into empty summer homes or relieve monotony with boisterous beer parties. Stopping drunken drivers and searching vehicles for drugs can be a risky business. Yet Jackson, who stems from a hardy old Ocracoke family, has the kind of physique that compels respect; he seldom needs to draw a gun. Moreover, he knows the usual suspects among the villagers and recognizes their cars and pickup trucks.

Jackson says that one of Ocracoke's oddities is that some outsiders come off the ferries blithely believing that the place exists in some kind of limbo exempt from mainland laws. They celebrate by driving 90 m.p.h. and brazenly indulge their drug habits. In response, the Hyde County sheriff's department was forced to build an island jail, set in a modern structure on the northern fringe of town. Faced with wood, the building blends well with the rustic village atmosphere.

131

Ocracoke

From outside it looks as though any prisoner could carve his way out with a penknife, but its separate cells for men and women are lined with concrete. Sometimes the jail is filled with overnight detainees — mostly drunks. Often Jackson has to escort a prisoner on the ferry to Swan Quarter for continued detention and trial, for there is no courthouse on Ocracoke. But he is an amiable sort whose round, smiling face betrays little of his sense that he is overworked and underpaid.

❦

My family, the Jacksons, are among the early settlers of Ocracoke and I've lived here all my life. Went to school here, worked at the Community Store, then had a couple of years with the National Park Service. And I had what was then the Exxon service station. Then in 1980 I took an eight-week basic law enforcement course at the College Albemarle in Elizabeth City. I've added on through the years by going back and taking other courses. Sheriffs are elected officials who aren't required to have any basic law enforcement training. But the deputies, who are appointed by the sheriff, must have the training and my deputy, Kevin Cutler, is in basic training right now.

Ocracoke is a full-time job for two men. I'd certainly like to see a third man. The winter months, it's not too bad. Summertime, it keeps you busy. We have different types of crime, nothing real serious like the big cities have. In the winter months a lot of summer homes get broken into, a lot of stuff gets taken out of them. Approximately 15 homes last winter. We don't usually know this until Easter weekend or the summer months when people start coming back to the island and find their cottages have been raided. Tools, fishing equipment, outboard motors, alcoholic beverages, stuff like that gets taken. It's mostly teenagers doing the break-ins and last year it seemed to be more than in earlier years. Before the package store opened they took alcoholic beverages and left everything else. Last year they were removing microwave ovens, things like that. We recovered some of it. A couple of weeks ago I investigated a case of break-in and found three men, all Ocracokers. The youngest was 19, the others 21 and 23. People didn't have to worry about this kind of crime in the old days. Years back, my family didn't lock up when we went out.

We have a lot of drugs and smuggling in the summertime. And there's a lot of drunk driving, speeding. They get off the Hatteras ferry and speed down and through the village, trying to make their appointment at the other ferry. It's nothing unusual to get out in the summertime during the day and cruise in with the ferry traffic and they're running 80, 85 and 90 miles an hour. That's all they want: to enjoy the beach and drink beer all day, you know, and relax. Along about one, two or three in the morning when the bars close and they go back to the motel or the campground, some of them don't even know where they started and we have to give them directions. We have to use a lot of physical force on different ones. They think the island is not part of North Carolina or of the United States; that they can do as they please. They just don't feel that any laws should be here. I've had them tell me that.

We patrol the island roads an awful lot in the summertime; as much as we can, the two of us. You try to rotate but you can't much, not just with two people. If I've got to arrest a drunk driver, I don't have anybody to run a breathalyzer test for me. State law says the arresting officer cannot make an arrest and run the test also. So the new man arrests the drunk and I have to run the test. If I'm off that day and he arrests someone, he don't have anybody to run the test for him. It's a hard thing to try to do with two people. We try to take two days off a week each, but it don't work out that way all the time. And for the other five days we're just 24 hours on call. We have to man the radio constantly. We don't have a dispatcher on Ocracoke, you know. My wife does a lot of dispatching. We've got a radio at home and all the calls come through my house.

If someone who flunks the breathalyzer test asks for a blood test, that's up to him. But we tell him he has to do it at his own expense, and it may cost him 65 or 70 dollars. Say we pull someone over for doing 90 m.p.h. and we bring him in and he fails the breathalyzer test. We call a local magistrate like Sygma Willis who comes around. His main purpose is to set bond. In respect of out-of-State residents you request a cash bond, usually 200 dollars cash. If the man can't produce the 200 dollars we keep him overnight. If he gets less than a five on the breathalyzer and can post the 200 dollars cash he's set clear till court. The court holds a hearing every two weeks [in Swan Quarter, the Hyde County seat].

I have less trouble now with local people driving drunk than I did when I started about eight years ago. When I started we had one deputy that worked by himself for approximately a year. People knew that if he made an arrest he needed another man to run the breathalyzer test. And that he needed one more to make two arrests. Now it's different, with the two of us. The sentencing, too, is getting harder. It used to be 100 dollars across the board. That was about it. It's gone up now; there's five different levels now for driving while impaired. It all depends on what kind of record a guy's got. It gets worse, you know. For a second offense now you get 10 days automatically in jail. A lot more money. They could revoke the driving licence permanently.

When I say there's less drunk driving now than there was, I'm not saying that they're drinking less, but they're driving less. This past summer they say there was a party somewheres every night. And I'm talking a party where there's sometimes 50 or 75 people there. And there's an awful lot of minors, under age, drinking. The drinking age here is 21.

You see children there — like all children, 14, 15 years old — that's downing beers.

A lot of tourists who come down here in the summertime bring drugs. Some of them bring it for their own use, a lot of them bring it to try and sell it while they're here. You walk through the campground, sit down at a picnic table or go into a tent; they're smoking marijuana, passing it back and forth among them. If they're smoking, and have marijuana or some drugs in their possession, it's an offense. The penalty for a guy caught smoking marijuana is 100-150 dollars.

If we find somebody with under an ounce and a half of marijuana, it's just simple possession. Over an ounce and a half is a felony. If we stop a vehicle and for some reason see residue or paraphernalia in the vehicle we search the vehicle and find out information on the vehicle traveling through. I can stop him and do what's called an emergency search without a search warrant. If I find over an ounce and a half I automatically can charge him with possession with intent to sell and deliver. If he has more bags with him, you know, with stuff like rolling papers or whatever, you take the vehicle. It all depends on how much you find. This past summer I found cocaine. And I found acid [LSD] in a stolen vehicle involved in an accident. The fellow thought he was flying an airplane! He probably found out that he was driving a car when he progressed a quarter of a mile and wrecked the car! Sure, it's an offense if a guy is driving under the influence of drugs. You see someone driving carelessly and recklessly down the road. You stop the car, walk up and the man looks impaired, acts impaired. You arrest him, bring him in, give him the breathalyzer test, he might have had one or two beers so he may blow a one or a two. But you know that he's impaired. You give him the sobriety test. He fails that. Maybe you find a little marijuana in the car. Some acid or whatever. You can charge him with driving while impaired by drugs, instead of by alcohol.

It's not unusual for the drugs to come in on fishing boats. It's been a couple of years now since we made an arrest for big quantities coming through. We had a trawler come through Ocracoke Inlet to Engelhard on the mainland, loaded with marijuana. The Hyde County sheriff's department, helped by the FBI and the Coast Guard, seized the vessel along with two or three trucks, a couple of cars and brand-new motor boats. We made 17 arrests. A sailboat that we got maybe six months or a year before that came from Aruba. It had three men on it and it, too, was loaded with marijuana.

We haven't had any big seizures of the hard stuff. But cocaine is the type of drug that you get a lot of information on its coming through — we stop a boat and search it. Because cocaine is so concentrated it's easier to smuggle. You can hide it in smaller compartments. The Coast Guard does spot checks on boats coming into the harbor here. They work with DEA [the U.S. Drug Enforcement Administration] and Customs. The Coast Guard and the sheriff's department work together real close here.

I got in the situation one time last summer where I had to draw my weapon. Thank the Lord I didn't have to use it. You have a split second to decide what's going on. There was a guy that was driving that truck with two others. I had one other deputy with me at the time. They were smoking marijuana and they had what they call a bowl, a water pipe. They jammed it down out of sight. I went to check the driving licence. The driver jumped out of the car real hyper, and as he backed off from me he put his hands round in back of him like he was pulling something out of his belt. I found out later that he had a bag of marijuana which he was shoving down his pants. You get people on alcohol and drugs and they just freak out when you stop them. We had a guy come out of one of the bars one night, stoned out of his head, and start shooting around in the parking lot. Just shooting

around wildly. But I've never had anybody shoot at me direct-
ly.

I wear full uniform in the summer time when I'm on patrol.
One of our cars is marked with "sheriff's patrol." But the one
I drive is unmarked, with a little blue light which we put on
the dash. The villagers back me up. For instance, if I'm
stopped at night on the road between here and the
campground, say, I've had cars stopped and writing people
tickets, I look around and see some of the island boys or
people stopped up the road to see that everything's all right.
It's nice to know it, especially if you're out working by yourself. You get all sorts of people through here.

There's a lot of times when you can talk things over and
work things out rather than arresting people and running to
court. We get fights at the bars in the summertime, you know,
that get nasty. You get a lot of domestic [trouble] in the summertime. Couples come down and the man goes off or the
woman goes off and one or the other gets drunk while having
a good time and when they get back to the motel they start
fighting, throw each other's clothes and everything out in the
parking lot. The man or the woman goes out, takes the car
and leaves the other one standing here. So we try to calm
them down. Most of the time the man's beating the woman
and when you go down and try to control the man, the
woman, she turns on you! That happens a lot. It's a
dangerous situation to get in!

Murder? We had a lady back in 1980, the first year I was
working with the sheriff's department, an 83- or 84-year-old
lady. The rescue squad was at the house and the other
deputy stopped by. They said that she had fell and hurt herself. The rescue squad had gone in and bandaged the woman
up and transported her to the hospital. When she got in to
the hospital the doctor examined her and he called the sheriff
on the mainland and told him that the lady had been beaten.
She was beat bad. She was injured a lot. She died next day
in the hospital. The FBI was called in, the State bureau of

investigation, they did an investigation on it. There were never any arrests made, but they were sure the lady had been beaten. All the good neighbors had been in just as she was transported to the hospital, cleaned up all the blood and straightened the house up. But that destroyed the crime scene!

There have been two cases of rape since I've been working. Both the rapists and the victims were outsiders. We've had no armed robberies. But we do get cases of fraud. A lot of checks bounce in the summertime. Some people try to defraud innkeepers. They get up next morning and skedaddle, skip out. But it's pretty hard for offenders to get off this island without being caught unless they've got plenty of time to do it. If we get a call from an innkeeper we get a description of the people or the vehicle and we just go right to the ferries. Or call the ferries. We work with the ferry people. We get them to hold the ferries, find the offenders and bring them back. The motel owners just get them to pay up; they're glad to get their money rather than press charges, take a day and go to court at Swan Quarter. This kind of thing is nothing unusual — it happens maybe a dozen times in the summer.

In the past I've had to call a State trooper in on a holiday weekend to help us out on traffic. We work all the traffic, we have to investigate all the wrecks — we have a lot of accidents here in the summertime. Litter is a problem. You see all the litter at the side of the road? It's a problem for two deputies to try to control it unless we actually see them throwing it out and leaving it there. But we can charge them, you know. As a matter of fact I talked to the sheriff today to ask him if he couldn't get together some of his 10 or 12 people jailed on the mainland for minor offenses to come over and pick up some of this litter.

Deputies' pay is mighty low. Starting salary for a trainee deputy now is $10,500 a year. If he gets his training within a year it goes up to $12,000. For the work we have to do it's hard. For the job you do, your life's on the line. I could get a call, walk out of this door and get shot in the next hour. I'm not saying the crime's that high. But you don't know who you're dealing with. You get a guy that's already been in prison and he's on probation for smuggling drugs, and he's got drugs in his stockings, that's a big chance you're taking. For our type of work, you know, the pay's not that great. The top pay for a man of my seniority is $16,000. But up on Hatteras [Dare County] a man with my experience and qualifications could probably make $3,000-4,000 more than I'm making on Ocracoke. Dare County's richer than Hyde County.

Back in May at the time of the crabfest I had a full house of eight people in the [men's prison] cell. The jail was used quite a bit in this past summer. Some of the local people got upset when we started to build a jail on Ocracoke. I don't like to think that Ocracoke needs a jail. But it's got to be the time that we do. I think anyone who would work with me for a week in the summertime would understand that.

I think in the future people are also going to understand that we're going to have to have a third man. Or auxiliary lady. Someone to fill in for us. We could combine sheriff's department communications along with fire and rescue. Also Park Service, filling in for them. A dispatcher in this building could also work as a jailer and breathalyzer operator. I would like to see that. I think it will come in a few years.

I've been out working from one p.m. till daybreak, seven a.m.; I've been working twelve, fourteen hours straight and then had to leave and drive [sic] to Swan Quarter with a man who couldn't place bond, and then come back and work ten or twelve hours. It's a pretty hefty assignment. It's a lot more than people realize.

139

Chapter 11

The Jill-of-all-Trades

Judy Ihle, a sprightly former flight attendant, is a mainlander who settled on the island in the late 1970s and became one of its best-known citizens. An energetic, curly-haired mother of two, she fell in love with Ocracoke the first time she boarded the Hatteras ferry. Although by now she seems to have tried her hand at most jobs, she is always hatching new plans and dreaming up new projects. A skilled handywoman, she wields a paintbrush and a trowel with equal dexterity.

One reason she is so widely known is that every January she acts as the island's official registrar of taxes for Hyde County. All householders must come by her place and sign up, which gives her an opportunity to exchange news and gossip. Then throughout the tourist season she works as receptionist at the Island Inn, another focal point for word of local comings and goings. She has also served as an agent for one of the biggest real estate firms on the Outer Banks. Her grown children both live on the island, one as a builder and the other as a hairdresser. With all this access to island news, Judy is a wellspring of information. A cheery woman, she spends much of her spare time tending her flower garden, riding her bike, or playing a weekly bout of Trivial Pursuits with her coterie of close friends.

❦

I was born on the Jersey Shore and we lived in a small town called Keyport, about 30 miles south of Manhattan. It was not quite beach, but it was close enough and we were beach people. Right out of high school I went to work for the New Jersey Bell Telephone company as a service representative for five years. And left there to go to work for Eastern Airlines for two years as a stewardess. They based me in Chicago at what was at that time Midway Airport. I married a captain with Eastern Airlines and he was based in Chicago also. I left the airline, became a housewife, had children. From the time Eastern sent me there, I lived in Chicago something like 18 years.

My sister Gloria already lived on Ocracoke, she came here in about 1967, when I was still living in Illinois. She called and said, you must come and see this island that Jack and I are living on. Jack, her husband at the time, was principal of the school here. So when school was out for the summer I packed up the two children and we came to Ocracoke. And then we did that many times, over many summers starting in about 1968. My very first feeling, I'll never forget it, was when we came down from the north, down through Hatteras. Just getting on the Hatteras ferry. And then riding the ferry across the inlet. It was, oh my gosh! I definitely had the feeling that I had come home — this is it! It was a gut feeling that had never happened to me in my whole life.

A couple of years went by, and I told my husband at breakfast one morning how I felt about Ocracoke. And I said, I know that one day I am going to go and live there. And he was just aghast! He had never seen it. He had never wanted to. There's not enough here and he didn't understand the

141

psychological appeal that it had for me. I mean, I knew that if I came here I would have to come by myself. And that was okay too. The marriage was already becoming rocky.

One year we stayed six weeks in that shack down there on the [harbor] point where the crab dock is. Right across from the ferry dock; a wonderful location. We had the best time! Life was just free-and-easy. We had cistern water in those days. When the power went out it didn't bother us. It was just like play. It was even better when the power was out. You really feel what Ocracoke is like, I think, when the power is out.

We moved to Ocracoke for good in 1977. The kids didn't come with me. Larry was by that time in his own apartment. Linda had two more years of high school, so she made the decision to live with her Dad. She was 15 and she didn't want to leave her friends. That's perfectly understandable. And it was okay. She and I have never had a problem. I built my first house here in 1978, paying $8,000 for a lot that would fetch $25,000 today.

I was fortunate in that I had some money and for about the first three years I didn't have to work. That was probably not a good idea, because I blew it! I didn't blow all of it — I built that house. But I played and had a good time until I got serious about life and decided I'd better go to work. Waitress, hostess, cook, cashier, you know, I filled in and then wound up towards the end doing all the ordering and the whole works. When the Boyette House [motel] was built, the fellows who were doing the carpentry work needed people to paint the sheetrock and everything. So we got together an all-female crew. It was like January, February, March, when everything was closed. I stained every bit of woodwork in the Boyette House. Sometimes I had four or five jobs going at the same time.

The islanders were friendly to me when I arrived, I think because my sister and her husband were here, and they were both heavily involved with the school. So everyone knew who they were, and when I was introduced around I was Gloria Tucker's sister. In some cases that made me automatically okay. In others it didn't.

When I went into real estate, that made a difference. I got into the real estate business at the same time as I started work at the Island Inn. It all happened that same winter. I went over to the mainland and got a real estate licence and went to work for the Midgett brothers, Stockton and Anderson. At that time people were already buying up land and houses on the island. At the [Hyde County] commissioners' meeting a couple of weeks ago they said 46 per cent of the tax dollars collected in Ocracoke are from "away people" who own homes or land here on the island. Another ten per cent are from people like myself who are not natives. So that's almost 60 per cent. There has been a great deal of land speculation here. Property values, they really have increased so much in the past 10 years, 20 years. Average property taxes more than tripled as a result of the [1987] revaluation. But if you compare it with the beach property business in Dare County or in Carteret County and then throw in the fact that we have 17 miles of open, gorgeous beach which nobody else has anywhere up and down, and the remoteness and reliance on ferries, which make it more appealing, not to everybody, but to enough, and throw in the fact that Ocracoke has less than 800 acres that can be bought and sold privately, then it's undervalued. It really is. But I don't like to have anybody hear me say that!

I think it's very difficult for young people to get established without being given land or houses by their parents. There's a man that I was talking to the other day who earns a living here on Ocracoke. He has a son and a daughter. He has a nice big piece of land. What he's really concerned about is, if the taxes get high enough, will those kids with their earning capacity even be able to afford the taxes on the land? You know, we're talking somewhere of a five and six thousand dollar tax bill. Possibly even more than that, if they improve it. Can they afford this as well as just being able to live? He has a valid point.

I've been doing the tax registration for several years now. All the householders come to me. And there's one lady that comes to mind that's been valued very high — she's on a fixed income — and her tax bill this year is going to run a couple of thousand dollars. That's an almost impossible situation for her. She doesn't want to sell any part of her lot, and she shouldn't have to. Sure, if she sold off one corner she could pay this year's taxes. But then, what does she do next year? I have suggested to some of them that they could give [property] to their heirs now and keep the right to live in it. And let the heirs pay the taxes and worry about it. But the tax laws make it difficult to give away a lot, and some of them are reluctant to let go.

Equity loans are not attractive to them, either. Some of the old people have never borrowed money for anything. It can be very difficult to borrow money down here, too. If you say a home equity loan, you're talking about going down to a bank, and banks have certain requirements about loaning money. They like to see central heating in a place. They don't really like it when you're living in an 80-year-old house, that's unpainted on the outside and looks like it's falling down. And you can say, well, yes, but I've got three acres of land here, with marsh here and Sound there, and it's worth 250,000 dollars. Not when it's under water, it isn't, you know. The banks are very, very conservative about lending money.

Some of the old people have been living in a house where all they've been doing is pay an electric bill and a telephone bill and perhaps gas for their stove and oil for their heating. And virtually no taxes at all.

People are comparatively poor here. I am! And yet here I am building a new house, right? I haven't borrowed any money yet, to build. There is no way I could live away from here and have my present standard of living. I know that it's not the jazziest thing because I've given up nightclubs and movies and bowling alleys and traffic lights and crime and all that sort of stuff, okay? But I really maintain that I have a pretty good standard of living. Sometimes I wonder how I do it. My groceries are relatively expensive and I'm single — I don't have a single dependent to claim on my taxes. And I can't file a joint return because I'm not married. But I don't need to spend much money. I have certain clothes that I wear to work. At home, I'm running around doing things, I wear things like this, I wear jeans, I put knee pads over them and I wear them until they're gone! I don't go out much. You see, after playing for the first three years I was here I got very practical, very frugal. I spend my money where it's important to me, and consequently I think I get a lot for it. I don't go up the beach [to Nags Head or Manteo] to buy cheap groceries — it's not practical for feeding just one person. But today Larry had a whole bagful of fresh crabs that he just caught, and I could have half of them. Anytime I want fish I just go see him.

I don't miss the bright lights a bit. I really don't. I think it's fun every now and then to go off [the island] and into a giant grocery store, especially when I haven't been in one for a long time. Wow! All the stuff! I can't believe it. Yeah, I miss theaters, concerts, libraries, at times. I get a bit of cabin fever from time to time, but not that often. When I was growing up we used to go to Manhattan frequently. It was only 45 minutes by car. Shopping, and having our hair done, and all kinds of things like that. And shows. It was great. But now I think I'm at an age where I am content. Because I did a lot of things before I came here. And I did a number of things even after I came — adventures which satisfied a certain memory bank!

If the oldtimers can afford to stay on the island, of course they will stay. And their children will continue to be here.

Ocracoke

They [the native islanders] call the shots. It's a very matriarchal society on Ocracoke. I think you'll find that in a family unit here, the women are dominant to a great extent. They are hardworking. The men are hardworking, too, but they also drink a lot. I think there's rampant alcoholism, I really do. I have learned to take it all with grain of salt. I'm an outsider, I'll always be an outsider. My kids will probably always be outsiders — maybe not my daughter. I don't know. She might bridge that gap, but I'm not so sure she wants to.

These people are Outer Bankers, okay? A lot of their thinking has come down from greatgrandparents and grandparents. In order to survive out here on this sandbar as long as they had those units as families, they had to have their thinking set in concrete. Many of them are very nice. Good people. Well, how can I say it? I want to say a lot of things but I don't know if I should! Basically they have been very good to me. I don't socialize with Ocracokers on a personal basis. It works both ways, I'm sure. And yet I mean, we speak if we go into the grocery store or the post office or whatever.

Certain fishermen do say "hoi toide" and people say it goes back to Elizabethan English. But I've come to think of it as just an Outer Banks-type accent. You'll hear it up in Dare County, and you'll hear it down among the Core Sands people, too. Even more so, in fact. They sound, some of them, almost like they had a mouth full of marbles. Where they roll everything around!

But there is a difference, culturally [between mainlanders and Ocracokers]. A lot of the people at times can be very narrow-minded, to my way of thinking. If you come down, as I did ten years ago, and you don't work and build a house, you're suspect. I mean, where does a woman come up with that kind of money, you know! And I know, because I got the feedback from it. It wasn't very pleasant. Of course, it's nobody's business. But that feeling does permeate a lot of things at times.

146

They don't have a lot of influence when it comes to running things. They've let the George Rutledges take it. And that's fine. George has done a fine job. I think that's what's going to happen. They're going to sit back here and grouch and complain about how Ocracoke is changing, and yet they don't do anything about it or band themselves together. I think their influence is diminishing as this process goes along. Yet at home, and on a personal basis, they still call the shots. I see the children in school that are the children of native Ocracokers coming along with the same type attitudes that their parents had.

Tourists — you just tolerate them in the summer. Everybody feels that way, and so do I. 'Let'em all go home for 24 hours, so I can get to the post office without being run over!' Things like that, you know. But the kids mean it, and they get that from their parents. I could give you some instances. But if it weren't for tourism down here, and the injection of new outsiders like myself who stay here, pay taxes, spend money and go to work in some of these businesses in capacities that they're not capable of working in, the economy wouldn't have grown the way it has. It will be true of the younger generation, too, unless they go away to college. And then they will see the difference.

There are some people who think the island school prepares the kids for life away. But I feel it depends upon the family that the children come from. There's a young boy now, who just graduated last year and started at the University of North Carolina, Chapel Hill. He's very smart. If anybody's going to make it, he will. He'll be an exception, though. And he'll do it because he has the parents for it. But too many of the children are either not encouraged to go away or they have just been raised with this outlook that, 'this is okay here and you don't need anything else.' There are kids who have gone away to [college] and within a couple of weeks they're back home. They're not encouraged to stick it out. I wouldn't have sent my kids to school here. When Linda decided at the age of 19 to come here, I tried very hard to discourage her. And her father was very much against it, and I thought that would persuade her. But she was that determined. So there was no point except in accepting gracefully that she was going to do it. Larry came about a year after she did, and he was at a point in his life where it was a good move for him to make. But he's ready to go away now.

I think part of the reason so many of the young people are content to remain here is the laid-back way of life. Also the fact that Mama will take care of them, you see! They are living at home. They don't have to go anyplace. They can get to be 65 years old and still live here. They don't have to do anything. Unemployment benefits are paid through the winter to summer season employees if no other work's available. But you don't collect the same amount of money you would ordinarily make. Unemployment here probably runs to 90 per cent in the winter. Everybody just picks up whatever little jobs come along.

I evacuated one time in a hurricane. The rest of the time I stayed. I don't keep stocks of food and water. If you know the storm is coming, then you fill up a few jugs of water. And you clean up the porch and the yard and get stuff in so it won't fly around. I cook up some chicken ... I don't tape the windows. I did one time and I'll never do it again, 'cos the sun came out next day and it baked the gook on the windows, and then you work the whole week to get the damn stuff off!

Chapter 12

Lord of the Manor

Colonel Wesley Egan and his wife own the Berkley Center, a small country inn they lovingly restored with carved woodwork and antique furniture. Discreetly screened by trees and lawns from the busy Silver Lake fishing piers, their hotel attracts visitors who care more for atmosphere and character than for standard motel decor. A tall figure with an imposing presence, the colonel seems somehow out of scale with the rest of Ocracoke. But he is an amiable innkeeper whose unhurried manner belies his former high-pressure career as a pilot and Pentagon official.

Like George Rutledge and other successful mainlanders who have come to Ocracoke, Col. Egan does not flaunt his background. A warm host, he is happy to chat with his guests and describe the legendary Sam Jones, builder of the Berkley Center. He also is delighted to show visitors around his appealing inn with its fir, cypress, and cedar panels on walls and ceilings, its fireplaces and its lookout tower that affords a panoramic view over Ocracoke Inlet.

❦

Ocracoke

This place used to be called the Berkley Manor, built by Sam Jones in the 1950s around and above the old Fulcher house that stood on this site. Sam Jones was from Swan Quarter, you know. And let me tell you a story told me by George Davis, who was a boyhood friend. And I can't vouch for its accuracy because Mr. Davis was about 80 at the time. But it seems that he and Sam got into a fight with a Negro and Sam hit the Negro with a two-by-four and knocked him unconscious. And thinking that he'd killed the man, Sam ran home and told his mother he needed five dollars to get out of town. And he did, and he went to Wilmington. Mr. Davis said Sam apprenticed himself to a German toolmaker there. (This was prior to World War One.) And after a while Sam said, 'Well, I've learned everything the old Dutchman can teach me,' and so he went to Norfolk. The Berkley Machine Works and Foundry there was owned by a very old man whose family had no interest in the business. And Sam went to work there and the old man liked him and kept giving him parts of the company, and eventually when he died Sam ran all the company.

So Sam became a wealthy man and he built six places on this island. According to hearsay, he would do such things as hide the beer under the cargo on the barges so that the men would have to unload all the lumber for his buildings before they could get at the beer! I think Sam did most of this construction to give employment to island people. After the Navy left in 1945 there was nothing on Ocracoke. I'm not saying he was altruistic; he had uses for his buildings. But he could have put them almost anywhere. And he was quite a man. You either liked him or you didn't. (I never met him.) The controversy over his jailing still goes on. I don't know the pros and cons, but essentially the government was questioning how he wrote off the cost of these buildings. You can get either side of the story from people here.

We discovered Ocracoke in 1957. I was stationed on Long Island at the time and we decided to go camping at Hatteras.

We came down to Ocracoke and at that time a Mr. Peele had a small ferry that would bring you over here and put you out on the beach. He could carry only four cars. There was no road — you were on a sand track for about the first six miles and then you were on PSP [pierced steel planking] until you reached the town. Then you were on the old Navy 10-foot concrete roads. To avoid getting stuck on that sand road you just kept going very rapidly!

We liked Ocracoke. Of course, we didn't stay that time, but from then on we came down year after year and stayed in various motels. We used Ocracoke as a pressure relief valve. All my assignments in the Air Force were high-pressure jobs.

We bought this place in 1979. We didn't start out to go into the hotel business; we planned to go into the conference center business. But 25 per cent interest rates in the late 1970s and early 1980s caught up with us and we had to start operations in 1982, sooner than we wanted to. It took us three years to remodel, get the equipment and turn the place into a hotel. We're still working on that, and it's involved a big investment. We still have conferences, however, and we're going after more and more. We're enlarging the place. We're in the black this year — it's taken five years.

Revaluation has increased my taxes by 250 per cent. But my complaint is not with the amount of tax but with the amount of good Ocracoke receives from the county. Less money is spent over here than in any comparable area on the other side [the mainland]. We should, number one, have more roads. I think the roads need to be maintained in better shape. The road to Oyster Creek is a disaster. Somebody's gonna get killed on one of those bridges. We had one car go over this summer — luckily somebody was there and rescued the young people who were in it. We should have more support for our medical service because we are more isolated than any other part of the county. We should have a county-provided helicopter service. I feel that our school could profit from a little more money, although they do very well on what they have and turn out some very fine young people.

Even after the revaluation, many of the older properties on Ocracoke are still rated low. My argument with the way they did the tax is that they [the majority of the Hyde County commissioners] are playing politics, pushing Ocracoke around to their own advantage. Only one of the five commissioners is from Ocracoke. They devalued the farmland in the county, which I don't think is justified. They devalued Engelhard, they devalued the property up on Lake Mattamuskeet, whereas they revalued property upwards over here because of the increase in tourism and because people have been ambitious about keeping it nice.

I don't think that's proper. But to be frank, it would take many hours of research by a real knowledgeable person to go through the comparables and come up with an argument on the sale of property. Now, property is not selling for low money over there and a lot of it is held by large corporations, in whose interest it was to devalue the property for tax purposes. A large part of it is corporation-owned farms. These people benefited greatly. The lumber people benefited. Yet lumber hasn't gone down in price. I try to get people interested. The only way is to get the town energized with facts and to go over and lay it on the county commissioners.

I don't think young people are being driven off the island by rising property valuations and taxes. I feel that if this were the case, then the older people would be giving them property. But they're not. The older people are selling to *auslanders* like us! The young islanders have got a very good education and if they want to stay here they can earn enough money to stay and buy property. They are making just as much money as the young people who have come to the island and done quite well as merchants or service people.

We have our lazy people on Ocracoke. We have people who use fishing as an excuse to get out on the water and lay back. But that's not true of all fishermen. There are also people who are escaping from the pressure of the mainland. We have a lot of those. They are intent on keeping the kind of laidback atmosphere we have — which I am, also. It's nice. I think we need to work at maintaining it. Not by laws and regulations. But we need to invite people down here that think the same as we do.

Much as I think we have to keep the island this way if we can, more tourist development is inevitable. Look up north: we have to recognize that places like Nags Head are gone [as unspoiled resorts]. I call them Pizza Alley and the Hamburger Hamlet. And there are many people who used to love that area and now that it no longer exists they are coming down south. Rodanthe is going to disappear. Avon has started to disappear. Hatteras has just doubled its water system — that's inevitably going to lead to development. Buxton, the same situation.

Our main concern is to keep them from building a bridge over here [from Hatteras]. There have been politicians and officials in the State government and the Transportation Department and up in Dare County who have suggested that. I don't want to give the impression that the Transportation Department is for it — although frankly I think they've done a study on it, but they won't admit it. We do have the National Park Service on our side. And there's no pressure from any real estate developer to try to upset the National Seashore. I think it's well entrenched.

If there were a bridge there might well be enough traffic to justify the fast-food or motel chains setting up here. And it would be a much shorter bridge than the one at Oregon Inlet, since Hatteras Inlet is a very small channel. We have a spit that they could bridge on over the channel. The trouble with the Oregon bridge is that the piers in the inlet are being undermined by the direct current and sink all the time. You wouldn't have that problem at Hatteras since you could span the inlet without piers.

153

Ocracoke

Do you realize that a lot of the traffic on the Hatteras ferry is one-day trippers: people from Nags Head who come down, look round Ocracoke and fish, then go back up at the end of the day? We don't benefit from those people at all. Many of them don't even come down into the village. They stay up on the seashore, fish at the northern end of the island and drive their four-by-fours over the beach.

I have no problem with the four-by-fours when they stay where they're supposed to be. But I saw one youngster at the wheel of a four-by-four go right up one of the new dunes we've had built, diagonally. He was gone before I could catch him. I'd have chewed him out. These are the people we've got to get after, and those who are drinking and driving. Maybe it's a question of money, but I think the Park Service should have a much more active police patrol on the beach. However, I think the majority of the four-wheel-drive people come here to surf fish. They're not the youngsters charging over the dunes, they're just using their vehicles to come to the beach.

We should avoid putting all our transient facilities, motels, restaurants and so on, around [Silver Lake] here, and killing the lake. One thing we might consider is what Bermuda has done, where they've put the transient facilities out in residential areas. Anybody who's been to Bermuda has to realize that Bermuda has kept its character. They're doing it by getting small facilities, staying away from the extremely large ones.

People in Oyster Creek will probably kill me for saying this, but we should have some sort of transient facility out in the Oyster Creek area. Motel, condominiums, something. Also at Springers Point [close to the lighthouse], but retaining its character. Getting small facilities is not inexpensive, but people will pay the price.

Martha's Vineyard has managed to keep people in there, or to get outsiders in. Artists, for instance, who fix up a little cottage very nicely. I think what we're going to lose is our rental cottage industry. That's going to keep going down and down, because people are going to buy those cottages to make very nice, small living quarters. We see a lot of yuppies here who like the laidback atmosphere. That's the reason they come. These are people we should encourage, and say, 'Hey, why don't you buy this little cottage and fix it up? You could rent it if you want. And you can get good rentals. Instead of renting to people who will damage your property, you can rent to people who'll take care of it.'

We're like the outside air in a steam boiler plant. The steam exhausts out of the valve; we can't control it. And the pressure is down in the boiler, and Nags Head and Greenville and Raleigh and Greensboro, Charlotte — they're the tanks creating the pressure. People want to get away from those places. More and more people want to find unspoiled areas. This is the pressure that Ocracoke is going to have to work against. But you can't really control it.

We should develop the airstrip because that would bring in the caliber of people that will want to retain Ocracoke. There is a building program for it. Frankly we do need to provide some fuel services from the town here, because people are flying dangerously [low on fuel]. We should keep it small, but put nice facilities here. So that people flying in here — and they normally bring their families — will say, well, that's a very nice little airport. Those are the kind of people that you'll find on bicycles once they're here. Most of the people we have here at the Manor, they park their cars and rent bicycles.

I was not thrilled to see the Anchorage Inn built, nor that place across the water [the Pirate's Quay residential hotel]. I was very happy to see us pull a height limitation. Scott Cottrell is running a very successful motel [the Anchorage Inn]. But I'm not in competition with him because I have a completely different type of operation. Most of the people who go to Scott had been coming to the island anyway. They used to stay at other motels. They want a view of the harbor. He has not brought a change in the character of the visitors to Ocracoke. The only people who appear to have lost out with Scott are the fishermen — he doesn't encourage fishermen and other motels do.

More and more of the younger people are getting to be managing things on this island. I don't think the old people really have the control they used to have. Now socially you may find it stratified. But I think you'll find that more and more of the control is exercised by people who either left the island and came back or have come to the island from other areas. Many of the older families went away. And the younger people that went away, who were in the Coast Guard or went to college or somewhere else, have come back to run things. Alton Scarborough, Alton Ballance, Dave Esham. And some have come from the mainland. Our water plant manager, Frank Wardlow, is not an island man. Yet he's had a great effect on the island. He helped develop the water system ... encouraged the health clinic. Jack Willis was instrumental in our school system. Jack and Frank were not island men, but they had immense impact on this island.

Chapter 13

The Builder

Craig Garrish is a sturdy young man who traces his island ancestry back to 1787. The name Garrish has a proud history on Ocracoke, bound up with seafaring and commerce down the ages. Craig himself was born and raised on the island, attended the local school, and soon became a civic leader. A prominent builder who runs his own business, he is widely liked and respected despite — or perhaps because of — his somewhat reserved nature.

❦

I think this place will go on growing, becoming more cosmopolitan with more outsiders. There'll be winds of change from the outside. I don't mind it; I welcome it. I decided a long time ago that we're going to change no matter what. I don't think you have to limit it — you just need to influence how it changes. It's still a small island. Eventually you're going to come to the point where there's as many people as can live here. Then Ocracoke's going to lose some of its charm. Some people will leave, and it'll start to go back. But right now it'll take a fair number more, and of course when people come, they bring stuff with them. And that is really good for the island, since it brings more work. There's a lot more developable land on this island that still remains to be built upon than you'd think. I'm just guessing, but I'd say between a third and a half. If you had an aerial view you'd see. So I don't think we're going to run out of land — maybe that will come in my grandson's time, but even then there's still going to be business.

Speculative building has picked up in the last couple of years. This is a big change. I don't do it myself. You've got to have a lot of money and a good credit rating to be able to cover it. It's easier [for the builder] because you don't have to deal with the customers. You just go ahead and build it the way you want it, then sell it. You can really make more money that way. But you're taking a chance. At the same time most people that come down here to build custom homes are acquiring a second home and they're financially secure. They've probably had three or four houses before and they know what they want. I recommend that they go to an architect and give them the name of a guy up in Chapel Hill. They can go to anybody they want, it doesn't matter. I give them an idea of what materials they should use.

Because of the hurricane danger we use special building methods. It's not so much anything specified by code. But we use pilings where other places use slab foundations, and we go seven or eight feet down. We tie everything together: the girders have to be bolted to the pilings and the floor joists have to be tied to the girders with metal tiedowns. The rafters, too, are tied to the top part of the wall with metal. One thing I recommend is to use half-inch plywood sheeting instead of something like compressed paper sheeting. And the houses I've built haven't suffered any damage from hurricanes. Look at this one: I think there were three or four shingles that had to be replaced after Gloria, which was the worst storm in recent history. I stayed on the island through Gloria, in my parents' house which was built in 1956 or something. My wife and kids left — that was her wish — for the mainland. But I had no qualms about staying.

With the rising cost of land you can't expect to be able to leave high school, get a job and immediately start building a house, or buying one. You have to work your way up. And of course it's a matter of choice. If you just want to be a fisherman, you've got to recognize that nobody's getting rich from fishing. Also you've got to realize that most of the income on this island is from the tourist trade. People are starting to take more advantage of that now. At the same time we're beginning to feel a little resentful because people with money are coming in and able to set up a business when islanders are not, you know.

There's some truth in the mainlanders' charge that many of the islanders simply work in the summer in order to draw unemployment pay in the winter. They're comfortable like that. I'm sure there are some people on fixed incomes who are at their wits' end to know how they're going to pay their taxes. They might have a piece of land that was worth $5,000 two years ago and now it's worth $50,000 or something; maybe they paid $50 taxes on it one year and next year they've got to pay $500. So it's stretching it for people on a fixed income. The whole Ocracoke economy, low or middle class or whatever ... the people have never had to do this before. And it isn't easy to get good financial advice on this island.

When I came out of school I was involved with the Civic Club and was president of it in the end. And I was in the fire department and things ... and it took me about two years to learn that once you get involved in something like that, they work you to death! It's the same people that serve on the committees and do everything. It's a lot easier to sit back and complain about what someone else is doing in a job than to try to do something yourself.

When it came to zoning, I supported their reaching some middle ground. I see a need for some form of zoning but I didn't want anybody to tell me what I could do with my property. So I supported the Ballance ordinance. I don't really like the Anchorage but it looks a lot better since they put a roof on it. It fits in more. At the same time I think they could have incorporated some wood to make it look more in keeping with the island. As for the high-rise hotel [on Silver Lake] — it's a very pretty building but it's too tall for that piece of land. I don't understand why they spent all that money on the building and couldn't buy a bigger plot.

The time is coming when we'll have to do something about a central sewage plant. The elevation's not high enough, so you're so close to the water table. It's getting so saturated that you're going to have to do something.

Looking back on my school days, there were advantages and disadvantages about the school here. I think that's probably the situation wherever you go to school; there are some things you miss and some you don't. You get a lot more individual teaching here but at the same time you miss out on a lot of the sports and arts and things like that which you can't get in a place like this. And I think it's ridiculous that the school doesn't even allow wives to come to alumni dinners! We argue about it every year.

I've never heard anyone talk seriously of building a bridge to Hatteras. I'm sure 90 per cent of the people on the island would be against it. Because now, with the ferries, we're limited as to how many people can come over. Build a bridge and it would mean people could zip in and out. It would ruin the island.

160

Chapter 14

The Sparkling Student

Cathy Ely, one of the brightest recent graduates of Ocracoke School, went to college on the mainland looking for wider horizons. A winsome blonde with a dazzling smile, she is a popular youngster who seems as much at home in the classroom as starring in the island's summer musical or working in a T-shirt shop. This versatile young woman enjoys sports, music, crafts, acting, and riding her bike to the beach.

During her school years she worked as advertising manager of the school newspaper and took advantage of the school's entrepreneurship program to start a business. Entitled 'Things to Do,' the venture sought to cure boredom among young Ocracokers by renting out games, VCRs, movies, and records. From Ocracoke she went to East Carolina University, the school of her choice, to major in mathematics and secure a teaching certificate. She was uncertain, at the time of writing, whether she would return to live on the island.

❦

Ocracoke

We were living in New Mexico and my parents got divorced. My mother brought us here because she wanted to be with her parents, who owned the Island Inn. So I was in the school here ever since fourth grade and I loved it. I'm glad we came here — I wouldn't have wanted to go to high school anywhere else. I don't feel I've been handicapped by the school. When it comes time to apply to college, you can put so many things on your record. Colleges usually look at all the things you're part of, and I had about 20 things on my sheet! Basketball, softball, school pottery, all kinds of art, drama. And you can get class offices real easy. If you work hard you can get good grades. You don't have to work that hard, but you have to work hard. You get your basics, your math, English, French, history, sciences, business — we have an excellent business class. You just don't get extraordinary things. And these other things look good when you apply to a college. They don't look at how many people are in your class. They don't look at the size of the school.

So I don't think I've been handicapped but I do think we need to do more extracurricular things in Ocracoke School. They're trying to get more stuff here, and I think they will, eventually. Last year they taught technology through the telecommunications hookup, with one teacher teaching five schools through an electronic chalkboard and speaker. This year they've added physics. Next year they'll add advanced math. Hopefully they'll have another foreign language.

East Carolina University is the only school I applied to. I think I want to go into mathematics and do something that involves computers. Or if I move back here, become a teacher. I don't know whether I'll want to come back here — I'm not planning on it. It just depends on what I'm doing in my senior year in college. Also whether there are any job opportunities here. Most girls who come back here and stay are married to someone here. Jobs for girls here are teaching or working with the ferries or maybe going with the Park Service. If you've majored at college in marine biology you can go into the Park Service. Or you can work at a restaurant or a boutique, something like that. It's boring, but it's a job.

Most of the young people whose families moved here from the mainland are ready to move out when they graduate from the island school. They're still used to all the conveniences in the city. But I've been here nine years and I'm not fed up with it at all. I'd rather stay. I'd love to stay. But I know there's no future here. I want to do something, to make something of my life. Some of my classmates want to do something with their lives, too, but they just don't want to leave. There are three girls in my [graduating] class. Myself and one of the other girls, we're going to college together. The other one, she's staying here. There's seven boys, and one of them's going to UNC [University of North Carolina], one might be going to technical school. Each year the proportion of people going to college gets more, I think. One's going to Nags Head and he's going to buy a car. Another's just bought a new car; he's got to pay it off and he can't afford to go to college.

It's comfortable living here, but it's not a very private life. Basically everyone knows where you are at all times. People always say that we're just like one great big family. Everybody knows everybody, everybody knows everything about everybody. This has its good points and its bad points [laughs]! One always knows when somebody's sick. When I ride my bike around the village in the winter, when all the visitors have gone, I'm waving to people all the time. I tell my friends that what I need on my bike is one of those little hands that go back and forth like this [gesturing and smiling]!

But you know what people did last night. I've talked with girls from the mainland who go out with a couple of dates in a week, with different guys. You couldn't do that here! No way! [Laughs] You'd be called bad names. If I went out one night with one person and the next night with someone else … you just don't do it! This is the most gossipy place in the world. Oh, so much gossip — too much, sometimes. It causes problems, not only with people of my age, but all the way up. That's something else that's always been here.

I wouldn't say there's a larger proportion of teenagers who drink here than elsewhere. I'd say drugs [drug use] is lower and I've never seen the hard stuff here.

I never watch TV in the summertime. In the wintertime I watch pretty much, since there isn't much to do. That's why we started 'Things to Do,' because we had no place to hang out. Every place we had was closed at night except Corky's. It has video games, a pool table and music. The Three-Quarter Time dance hall has a license and occasionally she lets us in — it's legal as long as we don't drink. We have more sense than to do anything wrong. I like to just go and listen to the band.

I like to go to the beach, but I haven't been in two weeks. We work! People come in [to the T-shirt shop] and say, 'why don't you go to the beach?' But we sit in the shops for them to come around and buy trinkets.

Eventually I think Ocracoke's going to become a resort area, to an extent like Atlantic City, New Jersey. I don't think it will be that built up. But the taxes are so high here that the locals can't afford to stay. We used to be a small fishing village. We didn't need as much. But last year they revalued for taxes and they tripled. And it's already caused two or three families that I know of to move because they can't afford it. And Ocracoke will be really quiet in the winter — like a ghost town. I hope this won't happen, but it's just what I see.

Chapter 15

Hutch Minds the Store

His real name is Cecil Thomas Hutcherson but everybody calls him "Hutch." Even his business cards carry the nickname. A cheery Virginian in his fifties, he owns the Variety Store, a catch-all emporium that sells everything from beachwear to foodstuffs and fishing tackle. He runs Ocracoke's supermarket as a family business and keeps it open all year, although business is slow in the winter. Its only real competition comes from the modest Community Store, the traditional shop on the waterfront that dates back to 1918. Hutch recognizes that the Community Store has many faithful village patrons, thanks to its history, location, and appealing Mom-and-Pop atmosphere. But when the summer cottages reopen and the tourists pour in, they throng his Variety Store with its bigger stock and easier parking.

Hutch is no Ocracoker but he came close to being a North Carolinian; he was born and raised in Halifax, a small community in southern Virginia less than 20 miles from the Carolina state line. He started in the supermarket business as a 16-year-old schoolboy working part-time in a nearby A & P. He rose to become manager of an A & P store in Virginia Beach, where he stayed 22 years. His purchase of the Variety

Store, on a tip from an Ocracoke friend, fulfilled a longstanding ambition to have a business of his own.

His round face flashes a characteristic wry grin as he describes the unique problems of running a supermarket on an island. But he has no regrets; he has done well from the outset and consolidated his position as the island's leading retailer.

❧

There are a lot of problems with operating on an island. It limits our deliveries, so it's a unique challenge. Most of our food, other than beverages, baked goods and dairy items, we buy from a firm in Rocky Mount. They have a tremendous warehouse with a big selection of groceries and meats and produce. We order by computer; everything has its own code number. They load up an 18-wheeler truck with a refrigerated section and it comes across on the Hatteras ferry. They don't come all the way down here [some 225 miles] just for me; they serve other stores in Hatteras and so on. If there's a storm and the ferry isn't running they just schedule the delivery for a day or two later, whenever they can cross.

Right now in the winter they are coming every other week. In the summer they come every week. And since we probably take seven or eight times as much from each delivery in the summer as we do in the winter, we actually sell roughly 15 times as much in the tourist season. We cut down our staff by half in the winter and shorten opening hours. But we still open seven days a week, even in the winter.

I put in our own emergency generator. It won't generate everything but we do have enough power to keep the refrigeration going and stay open. The computer and the cash register have battery packs we can use when there's a power outage. So we're pretty well insulated against wind and weather.

We know that the islanders have been driving up to Nags Head or Elizabeth City to buy their staple items — they've been doing it for years [to save money]. Food costs more when it comes off the truck here than it does, say, in Nags Head. They charge us a trucker fee, for one thing, to deliver across the ferry. Then we don't have the buying power that the big chains have. They can buy merchandise wholesale cheaper than we can because they buy in such large quantities. We're just in business to try to give people extra things they've forgotten to buy and they need right now. Of course, the tourists probably buy a lot more meats and groceries [from the Variety Store] than the local people.

If you want to get accepted on the island you've got to prove yourself. This is a pretty close, tight community. At first, people were feeling me out to find out what kind of people we are. And I think once people found that we were loyal and going to treat 'em right they did accept me and I've made many friends on the island.

I'm in business for myself now and I can indoctrinate my own ideas. Of course, when you work for a big chain you're almost dictated to in everything. I don't know that I do a lot of things different than I did with A & P. But it gives you a good feeling to be free. It's been very rewarding. Financially, we've been very satisfied right from the start. I think you get out of something whatever you put into it. And when you're working for yourself — I don't work any harder here than I worked for A & P. Probably not as hard, maybe. But I've got my children, they're young, they're eager to learn and I'm teaching them everything I know. My wife does all the book work [bookkeeping]. It's been a good team.

Not having a bridge is one the things that help to keep Ocracoke like it is. A lot of people have never been on a ferry before and enjoy the ride. It's really something different. There's not many places left that you don't have a bridge or something to come across. I think Ocracoke is going to stay essentially the same and change only very slowly. And I hope it will. I sure don't want to see too much commercial development.

I really wouldn't like to see McDonald's and Hardees and all those things. Not that I see much danger of that.

Part of Ocracoke's appeal is that we've got one of the nicest and longest beaches in the country that I know of — and one of the cleanest. And people want to relax, get away. There's only one motel with telephones [in every room] and people like this. Things are not too sophisticated. We like it that way and I think that's what brings people here. There's not a lot of room to put in new shops and motels. Building of new houses has certainly picked up in the last couple of years but I think it's reached its peak and we'll see a slowing-down.

I don't think outsiders are taking over the island and I don't see much danger that this will happen. Sure, property taxes are going up but a lot of young [island] people still seem to be making it. And the kids who come out of Ocracoke school and go to the mainland haven't had a hard time competing with the mainlanders.

Chapter 16

The Teacher-Conservationist

D avid Senseney, a towering figure in his forties with a shaggy black beard, is an immigrant from the mainland and a man with a triple mission. He is an innovative teacher whose methods include broadening the curriculum by means of a video teaching link with other rural schools and encouraging high school seniors to open small businesses. Secondly, he is campaigning to preserve what remains of Ocracoke's traditional village character by turning it into a National Historic District.

Thirdly, he and his engaging wife Sherrill have moved into big-time commercial real estate (by island standards) since they came to Ocracoke in the 1970s. First they bought the Community Store, which dates back to World War I and is a favorite haunt of old-style Ocracokers. Then they heard that a little old house that stood on the site of the present-day Anchorage Inn was due for demolition. They rescued it, moving it bodily to a harborside location next to the Community Store and turning it into an antique shop. Then they set up a hardware store and a T-shirt shop across the way, completing their purchase of a shopping complex in the heart of the village. It could be renamed Senseney Mall, but modest David Senseney shudders at the thought. In the summer he plays Blackbeard in Ocracoke's amateur musical, swash-buckling with abandon. With his hirsute face and stalwart figure, he seems predestined by Central Casting for the part.

❦

David: Nobody in my family had ever heard of Ocracoke before Sherrill and I first came here on our honeymoon. She was putting me through graduate school at the University of South Carolina, Columbia, at the time. I was actually finish-ing an undergraduate degree in psychology and doing a master's degree in community psychology. And I was doing an internship at a mental health center, doing crisis inter-vention work — drugs, alcohol, suicides, that sort of thing. Late nights, mostly. And we liked Ocracoke so much on our honeymoon that we chose it as a place to live for about a year while I wrote my master's thesis. We didn't really plan to stay very long. I'd been working as a professional with the Boy Scouts of America and Sherrill was in professional church work, teaching adults. We were planning to go back to South Carolina.

My father, particularly, was pretty appalled at the idea of my coming to this island out in the middle of nowhere. He didn't think it was going to do me any good. But we stayed. I was not trained from the start to be a teacher. I really got a teaching certificate just so that we could make a living on Ocracoke. Sherrill already had one, but she wasn't really a schoolteacher, either. Anyway, we started teaching school and it turned out that I liked it. I'm not sure that I'd enjoy teaching anywhere else, but here there's something different every year. I like to do new things, to set things up, watch them get going and get myself out of it, if I can. So teaching here is just fine. Despite its small size, the school here really does prepare kids for life in mainstream America.

Sherrill: I think kids have more opportunities because the school's small — for two reasons. One is that the student-faculty contact is so intimate. There are no students that fall through the cracks here and get lost. You know, that just kind of float through school and nobody knows them. Our teacher-pupil ratio — 95 kids this year and eight certified teachers — is one to twelve. That's better than anywhere in the State and probably in the U.S. The other thing is, because we are so small, we get a lot of special attention and funding, from the State, from private foundations like the Reynolds Foundation. We have more computers per child than any other school I know of.

David: It's true that I don't have a lot of lab equipment for my biology classes. But we live in a laboratory! Somebody from the fisheries calls up and says there's a unique specimen washed up on the beach. So we can load all the kids into the bus and take them there immediately. There's no bureaucracy.

Now we've had this telecommunications project for two years. It's an effort to bring subjects to kids in small schools that they wouldn't ordinarily be able to have. It's a State project in a pilot scheme that links an audio and a visual signal between six schools. We have a conference telephone and an electronic chalkboard. If you've never seen an electronic chalkboard, it's a plastic blackboard about four feet by six and you write on it with an erasable marker. There's a sensor grid under the plastic that picks up the pressure of the marker and turns it into a digital signal that is sent through a coding machine over the phone line. And it comes out in the other classrooms through decoders so that it appears instantly as a video signal on their television screens. I can draw a grid and, say, fill in one of the boxes and a kid from each of the other schools can fill in a box. It's totally inter-active.

At the moment it's heavily into vocational subjects, since that's where the money is. But I think it would be good for, say, German. We only teach French here. It would be good to use it for the languages we don't have the teachers for. It would be good for math, too. The beauty of it is, we can have one or two in each school interested in a particular course, and it's okay. If we don't have anyone interested in a given course, we just don't tune in. It's expensive — it runs three hours a day. Last year we had two kids who took physics with the help of this; the first time physics had been taught since we came here. And one of them is going to UNC Chapel Hill next year. Most of the kids who go to college go to East Carolina University or one of the technical places.

Sherrill: There's not much on Ocracoke you need a col-lege education for. Most of the kids don't want to leave the island. Their attitude is, gosh, when you live in paradise, why go somewhere else? [Laughs] I can't argue with that. I mean, we chose it as a lifestyle. The thing we think is important is for them to have enough education and enough skills that they can cope with living on Ocracoke and with all the pres-sures of development. Then they can have some control over development, rather than just being the victim of it.

I think this school can offer as good an education as any kid needs, and a more tailor-made education I don't know where you'd find. The problems that I see are not with the school *per se*, because if a kid wants a course or is interested in a certain thing, he gets it. The problem is mainly in the social milieu; the values that the families themselves have, and pass along.

At times there is a peer group pressure not to excel. Right now, we're fortunate. We've got a group at high school who are exceptional kids, and they are kind of setting a better tone.

David: One thing that's very clear about Ocracoke is that there really isn't much of a class system. The person who rides the garbage truck or works as a waitress in a restaurant or a maid in a motel is accepted all over the community. I think it's good. Isn't the school system set up to teach the values of the community? I think it is. And I think the school is doing a terrific job and probably is stretching the kids a little.

Our young people here are doing pretty well. Craig Garrish — how old is he — 28? 30? As you say, a builder, and not much more than that. Craig, when he went to university, he stayed three days. Or was it three weeks? Anyway, I gave him a hard time. And I gave Betty Sue, his wife, a hard time, trying to get her to pressure him into staying. And I was wrong. I don't think there's a feeling among the islanders of 'what's good enough for me is good enough for my kids.' But there is a feeling that being happy and contented and being with your family and taking time out to enjoy fishing and nature and each other is important. That's a lot more important than driving fast in the U.S. and getting a contract with some company to work for until you retire.

Sherrill: One of the real doubts I had about living here longer than one year was whether it would be interesting enough for me, intellectually and socially. And I'm just amazed. We have met so many more people here. I find that the local people are very intelligent and well-read, even though they may not have a college degree. And we're also meeting [mainland] people who love Ocracoke and come back year after year, really super people. I'm sure we'd never have been in the same social circles if we'd lived, say, in Washington, D.C.

David: We have another pilot program running in the school — I get all the pilot programs! It's called entrepreneurship. A guy who specializes in rural education and is pretty well-known nationally came up with the idea. His name is John Sher. Lived in Maine, California, Australia. Entered Harvard at 16, finished his graduate degree at 23. Well, John has the idea that kids leave small towns in search of work not realizing that there are opportunities available locally in terms of setting up their own businesses. John's idea is, if we teach them to identify local needs that are not being met we'll be able to retain them in their home areas. And we should teach them small business ownership and management. Ocracoke was chosen as one of the areas for the pilot program, as well as a very poor, predominantly black county up north on the Virginia line — a real desolate kind of a place. Last year was the first time we've done it, and we had two businesses come out of it. Whether or not these businesses survive, it lets us see how it's done.

Sherrill: The kids have to come up with the ideas, to do the research and determine what gaps there are to be filled with a business. And then they have to write a formal business plan. And analyze all the figures, determine how much money they would need and project paybacks and all that. And then we go to a bank or other lender and get the money.

David: We're still working on where they get their capital. Banks are pretty leery of this. We've not had any success locally. The start-up capital is foundation money, which comes from some of the big corporations and banks in North Carolina which like to see kids learning to start their own businesses. The money has to be repaid within a set period, so the kids have a deadline to make their business go.

Sherrill: They do get a little bit of grant money. Like when they finish their business plans they present them to a panel in Raleigh made up of somebody from the Commerce Department, a banker and a lawyer. The kids are cross-examined. And if their business plans are deemed acceptable they get a straight-out grant of $500. Not a great deal. Cathy [Ely] was just super when she went to Raleigh and was interviewed by this panel. All the kids were. We were so proud of them — that they could get up in this totally unfamiliar situation and talk intelligently and confidently about their plans.

David: Cathy and two of her friends started the 'Things to Do' business. The kids aren't old enough to enter into legal contracts. In the case of Cathy's business, they formed a partnership and the Hyde County school system is one of the partners. And Hyde County can enter into legal contracts with banks. In three years Hyde County has got to get out of it — that's part of the deal.

Sherrill: It's not completely the real world, in that neither the kids nor their parents have to carry the losses if a business fails. But what's been exciting for us is that for a long time we've watched these kids growing more and more bitter and sort of feeling a hopeless sense that they're losing control of their lives. And with just these that have been involved in the program, and others who have been coming along and watching it, there's been a big reversal. Whereas they used to call tourists "dingbatters" and complain about them, now they're talking about how they can get the tourists into the front door of their business. That changes their whole perspective.

David: Ocracoke has a village of character that most other parts of the Outer Banks don't have. There are neat little villages like Avon but they don't have the centralized harbor neighborhood that we have. I'd like to see that area around the harbor and Howard Street preserved. I think it's important to our way of life, important to the kind of people that visit Ocracoke and appreciate it. And I think it's important in dollars. There are people who are interested in old houses who will buy them as summer homes. So we're trying to get the old village designated a National Historic District, along with places like Georgetown [D.C.], Cape May [N.J.] and downtown Philadelphia.

A National Historic District designation doesn't impose any restrictions. It's not like our lighthouse, which has been designated a National Historic Site and has to be preserved according to national registered standards. There's a group from the National Park Service here right now, repairing the lighthouse keeper's house. And it has to be done authentically, to keep it in its original condition. It's an expensive thing to do.

But making a place a National Historic District doesn't tell anyone what to do. It just says that this is a significant area people should be proud of. And it helps the owners by telling them that if they want to restore a house in authentic style, this is the way to do it. It describes the kind of architectural details that should be used: windows, porch columns, roof materials, colors. It doesn't say that you have to use this type of material. You can put a tin roof on your house if you want to. But it does give people a 25 percent tax credit to do what's right and restore buildings according to these standards. What we're trying to do is to get a large enough district to include all the significant areas: generally speaking all the harborside to the Coast Guard station, all the streets from the Island Inn down to that point, all of Howard Street, all the back roads running from behind the school and the road running past the British cemetery, down to the end. The local State senator got us a $10,000 grant to run a survey. Consultants came in, looked at all the buildings, surveyed them, took pictures inside and out and did title deed research on their history. Now they're making a pitch to the State architectural review board that this is a significant district, part of our national heritage that ought to be preserved. I don't think there will be a problem. I think it will be approved.

Scott Cottrell's exactly right when he claims that he's raised standards with his Anchorage Inn. But he didn't need to do it with a big red-brick building. And he's made Ocracoke a more expensive place. He's forced other motels to make a lot of improvements which drive up their rates. He's attracting another kind of tourist. As for that Pirates' Quay Hotel across the harbor, it's too big.

It would be fine if it were built out here on the back of Jackson Tract. But it's jammed in a little lot. The lady who built it, Jo Everhard, she's a really nice lady who used to work for us in the 'Gathering Place.' When she originally bought the lot she wanted to build a really low-slung motel of natural materials that would fit in better. And she wanted us to help her furnish it with antiques. But she had to change her mind.

When the little house that we now have our antique shop in became available, it was where the Anchorage Inn now stands. It was going to be burned to clear the site and give the fire department some practice. But we were able to move it. Scott Cottrell [owner of the Anchorage] told me I could have it if I wanted it, but he said, 'it will have to be off of here by Sunday afternoon, because Monday morning we start driving pilings.' This was Wednesday! I called a man in Manteo, who brought two old I-beams that had been in a fire and a truck with dead batteries in it. Fortunately I have a military jeep I could use to jump-start his truck. One inebriated old man was his helper, and every day by about two o'clock he was worthless. I had to take the rest of the week off to help move it. But we got there, and got it up on pilings. We made it the 'Gathering Place,' a little antique business.

I don't think Ocracoke will ever be a totally slick resort like Hilton Head or Jekyll Island. Those were just barren beaches until people bought them and said, this is a development. I don't see this island attracting the chain motels or the fast-food places — it's too seasonal. And there's still an enormous amount of land here that is controlled by local people. A number of them you'll never be able to pry out of this island with a crowbar or any amount of money.

Chapter 17

Epilogue: Concerns of the '90s

Ocracoke in the 1990s is changing fast. Since the foregoing was written, the island has become a hive of political activism. Native islanders as well as immigrants from the mainland are roused as never before to take affairs into their own hands. Campaigns, petitions and litigation are mushrooming as Ocracokers try to get a tighter grip on local planning and to ride herd on developers trying to flout environmental rules. Residents of the Oyster Creek subdivision, irked by potholed roads and hazardous bridges, even threaten a tax revolt.

Little of this ferment is visible to the summer visitor. Tourists find the island outwardly calm. They also find it still pretty much unspoiled. To be sure, they discover each year one or two new restaurants, gift shops and bed-and-breakfast homes. They may see builders razing cedars and scrub to make way for more rental cottages. But Ocracoke's incomparable beach, wetlands and maritime forest remain apparently intact. Those visible changes that have occurred, such as the destruction of the tall dunes that formerly overlooked Ocracoke Inlet, were wrought more by Mother Nature than human activity.

Storms have been frequent, but Ocracoke was spared a direct hit from hurricanes in the three years since the first edition of this book went to press. Hurricane Hugo, the gale that devastated Charleston and much of the South Carolina coastline in September, 1989, mercifully missed Ocracoke completely. But another storm 13 months later severed the island's lifeline for months on end. It tore a dredger from its moorings in Oregon Inlet and smashed it into the Bonner Bridge, tearing a 370-foot hole in the span. Had this accident come in peak season, it would have played havoc with Ocracoke's tourist business. As it was, it was bad enough. For the bridge not only carries Highway 12, the vital road linking all the Outer Banks communities, but also the power lines serving Ocracoke. Fortunately the new Ocracoke generator could be pressed into service, but Hatteras Island was without power for several days.

The bridge fell in the early hours of October 26, 1990, and within hours thousands of motorists stranded on Hatteras Island started heading for Ocracoke. With their escape route to the north cut off, their only hope of getting back to the mainland was by way of the Pamlico Sound ferries out of Ocracoke's Silver Lake. And despite around-the-clock services, these four ferries proved no substitute for the smashed Bonner Bridge. Soon the lines of waiting cars and recreational vehicles — many with children aboard — were backed up through the village and far out toward the Park Service campsite. As nocturnal temperatures dropped into the forties, Marine Corps helicopters flew in blankets and 1,500 sleeping bags. Ocracoke families, the Red Cross, the Salvation Army and others provided thousands of sandwiches, hot drinks and other aid.

The Bonner Bridge was down for three-and-one-half months and cost $3.5 million to repair, not counting $20,000 a day to run an emergency ferry service across Oregon Inlet.

But even after the bridge was reopened on February 12, 1991, it remained in parlous shape. Jimmy Lee, head of bridge maintenance at North Carolina's Transportation Department, said the entire span would have to be replaced by the year 2000. Every month, divers go down to inspect the scouring effect of the shifting sands around the bridge piers in this strongly tidal channel. Lee said: "we are armoring the seabed around the piers with stone-filled wiremesh." In addition to this external erosion, salt penetrates into the columns and corrodes their steel reinforcement bars, which then expand and crack the surrounding concrete.

The bridge collapse came to Ocracokers as a stark reminder that their island home is much more dependent upon its lifeline up the Outer Banks (the short ferry ride to Hatteras and the road northward toward Manteo and Nags Head) than its distant links with the mainland across Pamlico Sound. And this awareness, in turn, helped prompt a campaign on the island for Ocracoke to secede from mainland Hyde County and join Dare County to the north. Ocracokers argue that it is an anomaly of history that ties their island to a county two and one-half hours' sailing time away on an infrequent ferry service. They note that Hyde County depends mostly on farming and forestry, which are non-existent on Ocracoke. But Dare County, like Ocracoke, depends on tourism. Hyde County, already one of North Carolina's poorest counties, has a shrinking population and tax base. But Dare County, which covers Outer Banks resorts as far north as Duck, is expanding and prosperous.

A door-to-door petition drive in early 1992 showed that 97% of Ocracokers favored transferring to Dare County. Four prominent Ocracokers, two men and two women, organized the secession movement. They argued in a circular letter to property-owners that "Hyde County has a limited tax base which will not be able to fund the needs demanded by our growing community." And they pointed out that a pending reassessment would probably double property values on

Ocracoke. Taxes would rise anyway, but in Dare County the tax rate was only half as high as in Hyde County.

Needless to say, Hyde County's four mainland commissioners opposed the secession drive, for if Ocracoke backed out they would lose their most vital and dynamic source of revenue. In this situation, the only way secession could occur would be through an act of the state legislature in Raleigh. And this, too, looked doubtful. Many state legislators fear setting a precedent whereby any discontented community could switch from one county to another.

At the time of writing, it looked as though the solution might be to merge small and heavily-burdened counties such as Hyde into larger, more viable units. As one local official remarked: "who needs 100 counties in North Carolina?"

Another movement afoot on Ocracoke in the early 1990s was to make the village an incorporated township. This would enable the islanders to run their own local government, levy some taxes of their own and spend the resulting revenue without asking Hyde County's approval. But Alton Ballance said shortly before his 1992 retirement as Ocracoke's Hyde County commissioner that precisely this was the rub: "many people fear that with incorporation they'd have to pay more taxes on top of an already high county tax rate."

As this edition went to press it seemed that the debates over secession and incorporation would continue for years before any decisions were taken. Meanwhile, the islanders will continue to suffer from the undermanned, underfunded administration run from the Hyde County seat of Swan Quarter, where key officials such as the county manager, building inspector and sanitarian work for a pittance. Given these constraints, it is small wonder that the issuance of building and septic field permits is a constant source of complaint. As the 1992 CAMA (Coastal Areas Management Agency) Land Use Plan for Ocracoke noted: "The effectiveness of both state and federal controls to protect the environment, in particular wetland areas, is being seriously questioned by a large proportion of the Ocracoke community. It appears that some development is proceeding in environmentally sensitive areas without the acquisition of proper permits. In other cases, there appears to be inconsistent application of permit regulations."

In other words, some developers have flouted the rules and been allowed to get away with it. But the good news is that more Ocracokers than ever — natives as well as comparative newcomers to the island — are alert to such shenanigans. So are CAMA and the U.S. Army Corps of Engineers, both of which are committed to protecting the environment. Increasingly, Ocracokers resort to legal action to defend their precious heritage against predators who try to exploit Hyde County's regulatory weaknesses. Many people hope that these village activists will win their war to preserve the unique essence of Ocracoke for themselves, their children, and their ever-growing influx of summer visitors.

Notes

Page
27. Account of Blackbeard's revels with his fellow-pirates is taken from Robert E. Lee's *Blackbeard the Pirate*, John F. Blair, Winston-Salem, N.C., 1974, pp. 89-90.

30. Arthur Barlowe's narrative of the 1584 voyage, reprinted in David B. and Alison M. Quinn, *The First Colonists*, selection of documents on the first English settlements 1584-90, N.C. Division of Archives & History, 1982, p. 8.

30. First modern spelling of Ocracoke appeared in *Colonial Records of North Carolina*, Raleigh, 1886-90, Vol. XVI, p. 75, in petition to General Assembly to create a new county.

33-34. Account of Blackbeard and his defeat by Maynard is largely derived from Capt. Charles Johnson, *A General History of the Robberies and Murders of the Most Notorious Pirates*, 1724, 4th edition reprinted by Routledge & Kegan Paul, London, 1955.

34. Gov. Spotswood letter of Feb. 14, 1719, to Lord Cartwright, Spotswood letters Vol. II, p. 272. Quoted in *Colonial Records, Vol. I* pp. 324-7.

34. For 1707 Act see *ibid.* p. 674.

34-35. Urmston letter, *ibid.* p. 763.

35. Hyde letter, *ibid.* p. 850.

35. Randolph letter, *ibid.* p. 547

35. *Ibid.*, Vol. IV, p. 1306.

36. Thomas Child, N.C. Attorney-General, letter of Feb. 25, 1752, *ibid.*, Vol. IV, p. 1300.

36. State population figures taken *inter alia* from W.L. Saunders preface to *ibid.*, Vol. V.

37. Sanderson will quoted in David Stick, *The Outer Banks of North Carolina*, Univ. of North Carolina Press, 1958, Chapel Hill, N.C., p. 299.

37. Dora Adele Padgett, *William Howard Last Colonial Owner of Ocracoke Island*, Port City Press, Inc., subsidiary of Judd & Detweiler, Inc., Washington, D.C., 1974. Her view is disputed by Phil Howard, a current Ocracoke resident interviewed by the author.

37-38. Lawson's *A Description of North Carolina* has been widely quoted, e.g. in *Senate Report on Condition and Tribal Rights of Indians of Robeson and Adjoining Counties of N.C.*, 1914.

38. John White's Narrative of the 1590 Virginia Voyage quoted in Quinn, *op. cit.*, pp. 126-7.

38. David Stick, *Roanoke Island*, Univ. of North Carolina Press, Chapel Hill, N.C., 1983, p. 246.

38. Burrington letter dated 7.20.1736 quoted in *Colonial Records*, Vol. IV, p. 172.

39. Dobbs letter, *ibid.*, Vol. V, p. 419.

40. Martin letter, written from New York in Jan. 1778, quoted in Walter Clark's preface to Vol. XIII of *State Records*.

40-41. *N.C. Gazette*, April 10, 1778.

41. Page letter of Sept. 26, 1777 to Gov. Caswell quoted in *State Records*, Vol. XI, p. 635.

41. Anderson letter of July 12, 1776, quoted *ibid.*, Vol. X, p. 662.

42. Pilots' petition quoted *ibid.*, Vol. IX pp. 803-4.

42. Wilson letter of May 20, 1778, to Gov. Caswell, quoted *ibid.*, Vol. XIII, pp. 132-4.

43. De Miranda quoted by Stick in *The Outer Banks of North Carolina*, p. 300.

43. Jonathan Price, *A Description of Occacock Inlet*, Francois Martin, Newbern, N.C., 1795.

43. 1810 official census.

44. Samuel A'Court Ashe, *History of North Carolina*, Charles van Noppen, Greensboro, N.C., 1908, Vol. II, p. 227.

44. U.S. House of Representatives Committee on Commerce report cited by Stick, *The Outer Banks of North Carolina*, p. 87.

45. Prisoners' description quoted by *ibid.* p. 128.

47. Ashe, Vol. II p. 670.

48. David Stick, *Graveyard of the Atlantic*, Univ. of North Carolina Press, Chapel Hill, N.C., 1952.

50. U.S. Lifesaving Service log, quoted in Nat. Park Service files at Ocracoke.

50. Letter from 1st Lt. Frank A. Newcomb, USRCS, Assistant Inspector, 1st and 2nd Life Saving Districts, to General Superintendent Life Saving Service, Washington, D.C., March 4, 1895. Nat. Park Service files, Ocracoke.

50. Letter from J.C. Cantwell, Sixth Life Saving District, to General Superintendent, Aug. 19, 1896. Nat. Park Service files, Ocracoke.

52. Letter of Oct. 9, 1950, from Mr Preston Basnett to Rep. Herbert Bonner enclosing petition. Bonner papers, Southern Historical Collection, UNC Chapel Hill.

52. Rep. Bonner's reply of Oct. 16, 1950, to Basnett's letter. Bonner papers.

52. T.W.Howard letter, July 4, 1952, Bonner papers.

52. Elizabeth Howard letter, July 4, 1952, Bonner papers.

53. Sara Ellen Gaskill interview of May 30, 1974, with National Park Service. NPS files, Ocracoke.

54. *Virginian Pilot and Ledger Star*, Nov. 17, 1985.

55-58. *U.S. Naval Administration in the Second World War*, Commandant Fifth Naval District, Vol. II, pp. 677 ff. Office of Naval Records and Library, Navy Yard, Washington, D.C.

58-59. Hatteras Minefield history, *ibid.* pp. 552 ff.

61. Sheridan letter, *ibid.* p. 508.

62. Lindsay Warren article in *The News and Observer*, Raleigh, N.C., Sept. 6, 1925.